STILL HERE
THINKING OF YOU

A Second Chance With Our Mothers

Vicki Addesso, Susan Hodara,
Joan Potter and Lori Toppel

ISBN: 978-0-9849567-7-7
Printed in the United States of America

Cover Artwork: *Mother Love* by Charles Frederick Naegele (detail)
Credit: Smithsonian American Art Museum, gift of William T. Evans
Cover Designed by Katherine Potter
Group Photo: Douglas Sarnoff

Some of the chapters in *Still Here Thinking of You* have been published previously:

"My Mother's Cookies" by Joan Potter – *Perigee*
"Outside of Her" by Vicki Addesso – *damselfly press*
"I Love You Still" by Susan Hodara – *Evening Street Review*
"Toothpick Girl" by Susan Hodara – *Venus Envy*
"Inwood" by Susan Hodara – *The Mom Egg's Vox Mom*

Boston, MA
www.bigtablepublishing.com

For our children

I have tried to unravel
The paths we've both had to travel
And now that I have come to see
How much you meant to me
We might get to see a better view
Yes, I'm still here thinking of you
~ Carol King, "Still Here Thinking of You"

When you still had your mother you often thought of the
days when you would have her no longer. Now you will
often think of days past when you had her. When you are
used to this horrible thing that they will forever be cast into
the past, then you will gently feel her revive, returning to
take her place, her entire place, beside you.
~ Marcel Proust, letter to George de Lauris, 1907,
   translated by Richard Howard

Table of Contents

The Writers

Joan

In the days leading up to the first meeting of our writing group, I was feeling increasingly apprehensive. As a memoir teacher, I'd helped others record their memories, but I had neglected my own.

A few months earlier, in the fall of 2006, Susan, a former student, and I were feasting on sushi rolls, sipping tea, and chatting about our usual topics—books and writing. I mentioned to her that, although I had been a journalist for decades, it had been many years since I'd tried—and failed—to write about my own life.

After lunch, I sent Susan an e-mail telling her I was so inspired by our conversation that I was ready to take a stab at personal writing once again. "I think I need to be in some kind of workshop situation," I wrote, "but I don't want to take a class."

"Here's an idea," Susan responded. She suggested we ask a couple of other women who had been in my class if they'd be interested in forming a writing group. And, she added, "I'd be happy to hold it in my dining room."

"I love that idea," I wrote. "Do you think we can do it?"

Susan contacted the others, and they said yes.

Nearly ten years before, soon after my mother died, I'd joined a workshop in which I'd written several short memoirs about her. But when the workshop ended, I put those pieces into a manila folder, where they spent all that time hidden in a desk drawer. Maybe I was ready to look at them again.

Susan

I liked that it was my dining room where our writing group would meet. On that first Thursday morning, I focused more on the others' arrival than on what I would read. I scanned the living room they would walk through, straightened the magazines on the coffee table, and hung up the jacket my husband had thrown over the back of a chair. I made a pot of tea and set out mugs, sugar, and spoons. I was excited.

I'd spent six years in Joan's memoir class, and for most of that time the stories seemed to pour from me. I loved writing memoir; I was pleased with my pieces, and a few that I completed in the workshop were published.

Then I stopped signing up for the class. I was building a career as a freelance journalist, taking on assignments for newspapers and magazines, and I told myself I didn't have time for both kinds of writing. But I also know that I had started to become oppressed by the obligation to show up with something to read every week. Now, after a few years off, I let myself believe that the mere existence of the group would be enough to make me produce good work again.

At our first meeting, we settled into what would become our regular seats. I sat facing the windows, fixing my eyes on the woods outside. As the others read their words, I sipped my tea and listened.

$\mathcal{V}$icki

I'd been through a rough year when Susan invited me to join the writing group. I'd been diagnosed with breast cancer, had a lumpectomy followed by six weeks of radiation therapy, and had surgery to remove my ovaries. I was writing in my journal, but the writing I'd been doing while in Joan's memoir workshop had stopped a year earlier, when I had to drop out. I remembered admiring the other writers' work, and their sensitivity as critics. My proclivity to see omens in even the most ordinary of occurrences allowed me to take Susan's offer as a sign. I agreed to join the writing group.

Wednesday came quickly; our first meeting was the next morning. The boys had gone off to school, Bill was at the firehouse, and I didn't have to be at work until ten.

But. The house was a mess. There were piles of dirty laundry on the floor, I needed to get to the grocery store, and I had so many phone calls to make. I remember thinking of my mother. As busy as she always was, she stole the time to draw and paint.

Because I hadn't worked on any new writing for our meeting, and was embarrassed to show up empty-handed, I decided to bring in an old story about being the flower girl in my cousin's wedding.

At that first meeting, Susan read first and her words were careful and clear, the writing crisp. Then it was my turn. I read my resurrected flower girl story, and maybe because so much time had passed, I thought it sounded fresh. The others gave me suggestions, and I knew I had made the right decision.

Lori

Late, I hurried through the living room. Books framed a fireplace and a beagle came plodding across the rug, following me into the dining room, where the women were sitting. I felt shy and nervous; it had been a while since I'd last seen them.

Joan was slender with short silver hair. Her manner was serene, but she had a quick wit. Vicki, smiling, leaned on her elbow with a dreamy expression and brushed aside her long blonde hair. Susan had brown curls, cut above the shoulder. She reminded me of a woman who'd belong in the Bloomsbury group with Virginia Woolf, something about her face, her pale skin, or perhaps because this was her house, and she had invited us to gather there.

I sat next to Susan, and we all caught up. I briefly mentioned that my mother had died the year before. We talked about our work, and I confessed that I missed being around other writers. Then we each read.

After two hours, I was back in my car, calling my husband. He saw the new writing group as an extension of my will and passion. I told him it had gone well; we planned to meet again.

As the months passed, how we were as a group was evident: polite, always grateful. We laughed together. Our writing styles were diverse: Joan was concise, often wry; Susan had an unforgiving eye for detail; Vicki's voice was lyrical yet unabashed.

My husband sensed my satisfaction. From the beginning, and every Thursday thereafter, he would ask me whenever I came home, "So how are your people?"

The Stories

*J*oan

Joan with her mother, Shirley Jean Propp

Opening the Folder

My mother, Shirley Jean Propp, died of congestive heart failure at home in Southern California on December 30, 1994, exactly one month before her eighty-fifth birthday. I was sixty-one, living part of the year in an apartment in New York's Westchester County, and spending summers in our log house in the northern Adirondacks.

Soon after my mother's death, I had an urge to write about her, an impulse that I can't explain. Although I'd been a journalist for almost twenty-five years, I had never attempted personal essays or memoirs. But now I wanted to draw upon my memories of my mother to recreate what I knew of her life, to express everything I admired about her.

I enrolled in a nonfiction workshop and began trying to tell her story. The teacher complimented my writing, but said he had the feeling that I didn't want to reveal anything my mother wouldn't have wanted me to reveal, that I wrote as if she were looking over my shoulder. He meant to encourage me to explore her story more deeply, but instead I turned to other subjects.

My sister Linda had mailed me a cassette tape a few weeks after my mother died. It was a recording made nearly twenty years before in which my mother had recounted many of her early experiences. But I didn't play the tape; I tucked it away in a box in my desk drawer. I felt I couldn't bear, so soon after her death, to hear her voice coming from my stereo speakers. But I also believe I was afraid to learn the troubling secrets that I'd always suspected she'd kept hidden when she was alive.

Months had passed before I felt ready to listen to the tape. I played it over and over, hearing many stories for the first time, and writing down every word. Then I joined a new workshop with a different teacher. Learning the truth about my mother's life allowed my writing to become more open, helped me delve more deeply into her experiences. The new teacher told me I'd made a breakthrough; I was determined to continue.

I spent that summer in our Adirondack log cabin; it was just fifty miles from Tupper Lake, where I'd grown up. I planned to devote those months to unearthing more information about my mother—discovering where she and my father were married, traveling to the cemetery in Tupper Lake where her father was buried, visiting the synagogue where I knew a photograph of her was on display, posing with a group of women from the congregation.

Most mornings I sat at my desk, spending much of the time gazing out the window. Occasionally I'd read my previous attempts at writing about my mother, change a few words, and return the pages to their manila folder. Then suddenly it was Labor Day weekend, too late to research my parents' wedding or visit the cemetery and the synagogue. Time to pack and return to my home in Westchester.

Once there, I continued writing for magazines and newspapers and teaching memoir workshops, where I learned about the lives of others. My folder of mother stories stayed in my desk drawer. But my path took a new direction in late 2006, when Susan, Lori, Vicki, and I formed our writers group.

I spent the first several weeks working on a piece I called "In Chemo World," about my husband's year-long treatment for colon cancer. It was later published in an anthology. Being able to complete this memoir gave me the confidence to attempt something I'd wanted to do for more than a decade. Now I was ready to tell my mother's story.

I opened the folder marked MOTHER, looked through the papers and photographs I'd collected over the years, and began to write.

My Mother in Tupper Lake

In the tiny black-and-white snapshot–a couple of inches square like most photographs of the 1930s–I'm four years old and posed next to a carriage holding my baby sister, Abby. She's propped up on a pillow, wearing a white bonnet and covered with a fringed blanket; one chubby hand is raised and her big round eyes are looking out at the world.

I stand gawkily by her side, dressed in a fitted tweed coat and a matching hat held in place by an elastic band that stretches under my chin, my straight brown hair sticking out at odd angles. With a finger pressed against my lips, I squint at Abby speculatively, probably envying her blue eyes and long, curly lashes.

We're in front of Cohn's drugstore, its plate-glass windows decorated with posters displaying stylish women advertising Old Gold cigarettes and Alka-Seltzer. My mother likes to take us out for some air every day, and we follow a familiar route from our house along the sidewalk past Mikell's market, the Moose club, Kiklevich's liquor store and bar, the lumberjack hotel, and, finally, Cohn's drugstore.

We lived on the road that runs through downtown Tupper Lake, which was officially called Tupper Lake Junction, because that's where the New York Central trains stopped. It was also known as Faust–pronounced *Fawst.* The wife of the Junction's first postmaster was asked to choose a name for the post office; she selected the title character of Goethe's play.

Tupper Lake was an isolated lumbering town in the northern Adirondacks; flat-fronted wooden buildings lined the few blocks of its business section. Lumberjacks left their camps in the woods and came to town on weekends, spending their money in the local bars. I remember holding my breath whenever we walked past the dark wooden hotel to block out the strong beery smell that drifted from its front door.

Sometimes on a pleasant evening when I was bouncing a ball

or playing hopscotch on the sidewalk in front of our house, my mother would appear on the front porch. "Come inside, Joan," she'd call. "Here comes a drunken lumberjack." I'd glance down the street at the rough-looking man lurching my way, and rush inside.

My mother was only twenty-one when she married my father and moved to that dreary town, where his family had settled in the early 1900s after emigrating from Eastern Europe. She met him on a visit to the Adirondacks from New York City, where she'd been living and working since she was seventeen.

She brought to Tupper Lake her youthful energy, good looks, and city style. Even to take a walk to Cohn's drugstore, or to stop at Mikell's market to buy meat and vegetables for dinner, she dressed well. In cold weather she wore a fitted wool coat with a high collar, a cloche hat tilted at an angle, and black leather gloves, and on summer afternoons she changed from her morning housedress into silk print dresses and pearl earrings.

I have photographs of her in those outfits, and I realize she could not have bought that stylish clothing in Tupper Lake. Maybe she sometimes took the train to New York to shop, or perhaps those were the clothes she'd brought with her after she married my father.

The images of her when I was very young seem to be a combination of old photographs and often-repeated stories. My actual memories appear in bursts, like the scene that's illuminated in a sudden flash of light from a camera.

I can see her dabbing on a bit of dark-red lipstick and smoothing it across her lips with the tip of her little finger, then patting flowery Lady Esther face powder over her nose and forehead with a pink puff.

I remember the stories she read to me from a big book with vivid illustrations: the pine tree with glittering glass leaves, the colorful cap and boots on the boy who herded goats, the rabbit who caught the sun in a trap.

She taught me to read before I started school, when I was not yet five. One day, as she told the story, she took me by the hand and we walked to the library to get a card for me. The librarian was named Florence Cheverette–people called her Flossie. Later she was my sixth-grade teacher.

"Joan is here to get a library card," my mother said.

"Why, she can't get a card until she can read," said Flossie.

"Well, she can read right now. Hand her a book and she'll show you."

I got my card, and we hurried home with new books in our arms. My mother must have been happy then. She hadn't yet been defeated by the narrow townspeople, my father's sarcastic sense of humor, the harsh judgments of his relatives. I don't remember her ever being mad at me, even when the elementary school principal called to report that I'd punched a girl who got in front of me in the water fountain line, giving her a bloody nose, or when a woman down the street came to tell her I'd bumped into her little boy while riding my bike down the sidewalk and ridden away without stopping.

She didn't even get mad when I was four years old and she came into my baby sister's room to find that I'd chopped off her sweeping eyelashes with a pair of paper scissors. She understood why I'd done it, and was relieved my sister wasn't hurt. "It's all right," she said, "Abby's lashes will grow back."

Spying on My Mother

Every evening, after she tucked me into bed, my mother picked up the child-sized wicker rocking chair painted pale green that was kept in my room. She carried it to a spot between my door and the room across the narrow hallway where my little sisters slept. She settled there with a book—she was so slender that she fit easily into the small chair—and read us our nightly bedtime story. When she was finished she brought the rocker back into my room and bent over to kiss me on the cheek, leaving a faint scent of her Lady Esther face powder.

When I was sure she was back downstairs in the living room with my father, reading or sewing, I got out of bed, inched to the landing at the top of the stairs, and stretched out on the floor, feeling the prickly carpet tickle my stomach through my pajamas. I lay there, breathing quietly, listening to the murmur of my parents' voices, trying to pick out enough words to make sense of what they were saying. Maybe they were talking about me or revealing a secret; I never heard enough to find out.

Before my parents came upstairs for the night, they sat at the kitchen table with cups of tea and cake or cookies. I heard the opening and closing of cupboard doors and the clink of a teaspoon on the side of a china cup. It was then that I crept back into my bed, where I continued to keep watch, peering over the edge of my blanket at moving shadows.

One shadowy figure that appeared every night was my mother. She tiptoed into my dark room toward the closet where she kept her clothes. There, partly shielded by the open closet door, she slipped out of her dress and underwear and into her pajamas.

I could see the movements of her body, reaching and bending, as she lifted the dress over her head and pulled off her stockings. I heard the faint click of hangers and the rustling of her bathrobe as she tied the belt around her waist. I watched through lowered eyelids as she turned and moved past my bed on her way to the room she shared with my father. Only then, when I knew she was in her own bed, could I relax my vigilance and fall asleep.

I spied on my mother in the daytime, too. When I was sure I'd be safe–she might be in the middle of cooking dinner or out in the backyard hanging clothes on the line–I'd walk quietly into my parents' bedroom. Their twin beds, separated by a night table, faced a heavy, dark, wooden dresser. The things I was looking for were in the bottom drawer.

First I took out the book–*What Every Young Wife Should Know*. I leafed through it, read some of the words; I think there were pictures, too. But the information it held was beyond my comprehension.

I put it back and carefully removed the shoes, graceful silver sandals with thin straps and high, slender heels. My mother once wore those sandals, I thought, and she also wore the two dresses she kept folded in tissue paper.

I eased out the dress that I thought was the most beautiful, raised it high in the air and watched it unfold. It was long and slinky, a pale, sea-foam green with a draped neckline and a back that curved so low that it must have reached almost to the bottom of my mother's spine. I envisioned her, back before I knew her, wearing this dress and those sandals, looking like pictures of women I'd seen in magazines.

The other dress was pretty, too, but not as glamorous. It also was a long gown, all white eyelet with black velvet ribbons around the waist and woven through the round neckline. Spreading the dresses across a bed, I managed to place them neatly into their tissue paper nests and tuck them away.

Eventually I lost interest in spying. But years later, when I was invited to my first high-school prom, my mother said she had just the thing for me to wear. I followed her into her bedroom and watched her open the dresser's bottom drawer. She lifted out the white eyelet dress and shook it gently until the scalloped hem almost reached the floor. The dress was still pristine, just as when

I'd sneaked it out behind my mother's back.
"You can wear it if you like," she said.

Joan's mother on the front porch of her Tupper Lake home

The In-Laws

We were crowded into the small, dim sitting room in the narrow wooden house where my grandmother lived—my father's mother—two blocks from our own home. I can still see her perched in a corner of the couch, a short, squat woman with a broad face, high cheekbones, and thick glasses, shiny scars lining her right arm where she'd burned it time and again stuffing sticks of wood into her black iron cook stove.

My two aunts were there—sharp-featured, red-haired Hazel hoarsely proclaiming her opinions, and Leah, tall, pale, and hourglass-shaped, responding in her fluting voice. When my grandmother spoke, it was with a heavy Yiddish accent, even though she'd been in the United States for decades.

My mother sat upright in a chair across from them, wearing a neat dress and heels, her black hair rolled in a bun. I knew she was unhappy to be there—I don't remember if she told me or if I sensed it—but my father's family expected her almost every afternoon to sit in that gloomy room talking about nothing important with people who looked down on her.

Later I realized that the two aunts, who were the children of struggling immigrants and had never worked or made any contributions to the world as far as I knew, felt superior to most people, and especially to those, like my mother, who had married into the Propp family. I don't know where this attitude came from. Belonging to one of the few Jewish families in a largely French-Canadian village might have made them feel special, but they also seemed to look down on the rest of the Jewish community.

Until I became a teenager and started living my own life, my two little sisters and I had to accompany my mother on those afternoon visits. While the grownups chattered, the three of us sprawled on the floor, paging through Aunt Hazel's shiny fashion magazines. I remember one day looking up at Aunt Leah to see her scrutinizing my mother. "Shirley, dear," she said, with fake sympathy, "you look so tired, poor girl."

My mother's lips tightened and she didn't respond; pink blotches appeared on her neck. I'd seen those blotches before when my mother was upset, usually about a sarcastic remark of my father's. She'd press her lips together and not say a word, but her tension entered my body, too.

My mother told me that before I was born she'd had to spend part of every weekday afternoon taking my grandmother and the aunts for a ride in her car. First she'd drive over to pick up my grandmother and Hazel, who wasn't married and had stayed in her childhood home. Then she'd steer the car three miles to what was called uptown Tupper Lake. Leah lived there in a big house with her husband, Uncle Frank, a genial man who played cards, smoked cigars, and owned the town hardware store.

After they'd all piled in, my mother would head toward one of the three roads that led out of town while her passengers gossiped and complained. One afternoon, my mother recalled, "Grandma lit into me for something. I was so desperate I got out of the car and was going to take off. I just couldn't stand it anymore."

She stood by the side of the road for a few minutes, she said, then got into the car and drove back to town. "I came home," she recalled, "and said to Daddy, 'Jesse, those people are driving me crazy. I can't stand it.' He didn't know what to do about it. They drove him crazy, too."

Aunt Leah, the older of the two sisters, rarely left her house except for the trips to my grandmother's and the car rides with my mother. She didn't drive, had a live-in woman who helped with the housework, and seemed to have no friends or interests outside of the family.

Hazel, though, sometimes walked over to our house for a short visit, and took the opportunity to check up on my mother. One day, when my mother was in another part of the house, I was passing our kitchen door and saw Aunt Hazel opening the cupboards and peering inside. Sometimes I saw her going through our mail before my parents had a chance to look at it.

My father also had two brothers, Elihu, who owned a printing company, and Simon, a doctor. They lived in Albany, but my father had stayed in Tupper Lake to run the two businesses—a coal and feed store and a bakery—that supported his mother and unmarried sister as well as his own family. The two uncles with their wives and children came up to visit my grandmother every summer. Uncle Eli was sharp-tongued and unfriendly, but I liked Uncle Si. To my mother, though, he seemed arrogant and haughty. "He thought he was God," she told me years later.

My father was different from the rest of his family, my mother said. "He didn't fit in. He didn't like them, none of them. And they gave me an awful hard time."

Only my father's father, Peter Propp, had been kind to her, she said, and he died before I was old enough to remember him. He had come to the United States from Russia in 1892, finally settling in Tupper Lake, where he ran a bottling works, then the coal and feed business, and was active in the community. My mother often talked about what a wonderful man he was, intelligent and cultured, even playing the violin.

In the late '50s, when I was married and living in the New York City suburbs and my grandmother was dead, my parents left Tupper Lake and moved to California. Occasionally my aunts called them, but if my mother picked up, after a few terse words she would hand the phone to my father.

It was a relief to both my parents to be across the country from Hazel and Leah, my mother told me. "Dad used to say, 'Thank God they're 3,000 miles away.'"

The Baby Boy

When I was thirteen years old, my mother became pregnant. She didn't tell me or my two younger sisters that she was expecting a baby. In fact, she had never talked to me about anything related to sex, not even to prepare me for my first period.

When I woke up one morning with spots of blood on my pajama bottoms and called to her in a panic, she led me into the bathroom, handed me a sanitary napkin and a narrow elastic belt, and showed me how they worked. She also gave me a thin booklet about menstruation put out by the Modess company. She must have said something, but I have no memory of her words.

As my mother's belly grew larger and she started wearing tent-like dresses, I realized she was pregnant. Maybe I knew this from something I'd read, maybe my friends told me. She switched between two maternity dresses: one was navy blue with white polka dots; the other was a solid chocolate brown. I thought both were ugly.

I saw no evidence of baby clothes or baby furniture; Jewish superstition did not allow such things in the home before the baby was born. One day, while wandering through my grandmother's house, I spied a white wicker bassinet trimmed with a wide satin ribbon in the corner of a spare bedroom. I didn't tell anyone I'd seen it.

Perhaps I overheard conversations about the pregnancy; maybe my sisters and I talked about it. But I have no recollection of my parents ever mentioning the fact that there would soon be a new baby in the family.

Early one morning, I was half awake in my warm bed when I heard my father's voice: "Joan, it's time to get up."

My father never woke me up. It was always my mother, in her housedress and apron, already wearing a bit of lipstick, her black hair neatly combed, who gently stroked my forehead and roused me from sleep. "Good morning, glory," she always said.

But that morning my father was standing at my bedroom door, dressed in a suit and a rumpled white shirt. "Your mother's all right," he said. "She's all right, but the baby died."

His words jumped around in my brain, and for one horrible moment I thought he was saying my mother was dead. But no, she was all right; that was the important thing. I didn't feel sad about the baby—I had been unprepared for its existence in the first place. Later I found out it had been stillborn, and that it was a boy.

The day was cold and rainy, and my father was out at the hospital and doing whatever else needed to be done. He said he'd be home for dinner, and I decided to cook a nice meal for him and my little sisters. I walked down the block to Mikell's grocery store and bought a pound of ground round—that was what my mother always ordered—and some vegetables.

At home, I spread the groceries on the kitchen counter and began to prepare dinner—hamburger patties, mashed potatoes, and peas. It was hard work; I'd never cooked a meal before. When my father came home, looking grey and solemn, I dished out his food and served it to him at the kitchen table. He pushed it around the plate for a while. "I'm sorry," he said. "I'm just not hungry."

I was sweaty, tired, and close to tears as I scraped his plate into the garbage. He must have been exhausted from lack of sleep and chilled by running errands in the rain; a day or two later he ended up in the hospital with pneumonia. My mother was still there; in those days women who'd given birth were kept in the hospital for a week. No one wanted to upset her by telling her my father was sick; they put him in a room at the other end of the hall.

My aunt was taking care of my sisters and me, and one day she took me to the hospital. My mother was resting on two pillows, wearing a bed jacket in light blue, her favorite color. "Last night I heard someone coughing down the hall," she said to my aunt. "It sounded just like Jesse."

Soon both our parents came home, and my mother repeated

the story. "I knew it was Daddy who was coughing in the hospital," she said. "After I heard him they had to tell me he was there."

The story was so striking that I have always remembered it. But if anyone mentioned the dead baby then, I've forgotten what was said. I watched my mother carefully for signs of unhappiness as she went about her usual chores—cooking, cleaning, washing clothes. She seemed the same, but for weeks I worried that something unexpected might upset her. What if she saw a pregnant woman in a store, or a new mother pushing a baby carriage along the sidewalk?

One evening, she and I went to the movies, just the two of us. The movie was called *To Each His Own,* and the star, an unmarried woman, was forced to give away her baby boy. I remember feeling tense and fearful, and I turned to glance at my mother, afraid she was in pain. But she was looking straight ahead, engrossed in the movie, the flickering light from the screen illuminating her face.

To the Rescue

During my teenage years, my mother was a figure in the background, busy taking care of the family. I knew that every morning, wearing a cotton housedress, she would clean up the breakfast dishes, run a load of laundry, and carry the wet clothes in a basket to the backyard, where she'd hang them on clotheslines bordered by a white wooden trellis.

After lunch and a nap, she'd prepare herself for the afternoon: a neat dress, stockings, heels, wavy black hair carefully arranged, lipstick, and powder. That was how she looked when she did her marketing and made her obligatory visit to my grandmother's house. By five o'clock she'd be in the kitchen again, cooking our dinner.

I don't remember talking to her much about my life away from the house, but in a small town like ours it was hard to keep secrets. She didn't have to worry about me, though; I was a good student, a cheerleader, and one of a group of girls who hung around together. There was always a boyfriend: John or Buddy or Donald. I knew my mother prayed I wouldn't get too attached to a Tupper Lake boy before I graduated and left for college. She didn't want me to get stuck in the town that she herself had always wanted to escape.

Yet she was always kind to the boys who came to pick me up for dates. It was my father, hiding behind his newspaper in the blue upholstered living-room chair, who made fun of them after I got home.

My mother managed to get the Sunday *New York Times* every week–ordering it from Cohn's drugstore–so I could read about the wider world; she wanted to show me there was a different, more exciting and fulfilling life that I could aspire to. Once, the two of us took the long train ride to visit the city. We saw *Pal Joey* on Broadway and ate at Sardi's, where I looked for celebrities and ordered a curry that I remember being a surprising shade of green. We walked around the city until our feet were blistered.

Tupper Lake offered few diversions for teenagers. We could choose to take part in high school plays, go to football and basketball games, or get involved in winter sports. My friends and I weren't a hardy group; we preferred to stay inside and keep warm. Most days after school we walked down the hill to Maid's drugstore, where we crowded into its red leather booths, piling our books on the tables and sipping our chocolate Cokes.

When we tired of Maid's, we went across the street to the Miss Tupper Diner, a small, narrow place smelling of grilling hamburgers. There we drank coffee and sneaked cigarettes, taking a chance that no acquaintances of our parents would push through the door.

The drugstore and the diner were our weekday hangouts. On Saturday nights we headed down the block to the Hotel Altamont, a rambling, four-story, white frame building that contained a large area called the Mountain Room, with a bar, tables for dining and drinking, and a dance floor. For our evenings at the Altamont, my girlfriends and I dressed in twirly calf-length skirts, short-sleeved sweaters, and black flats. My sweaters were snug, often fuzzy angora, and with them I wore a short string of pearls or a small scarf tied at the side.

My mother gave me permission to go to the Altamont as long as I got home on time—I think my curfew was 11 o'clock—but she sometimes criticized my tight sweaters. "You look like a chorus girl," she'd say.

What she didn't know was that while my friends and I sat around a table near the bar listening to music on the jukebox and hoping to be asked for a dance, we smoked the Camels we'd carefully hidden in the depths of our jacket pockets, and ordered rum-and-Cokes, even though none of us had reached the legal drinking age. Hanging on the wall in full view of our table was a cardboard sign with thick red letters that read: "No Minors Permitted in Bar or Mountain Room at any Time." The owners surely knew we were still in high school, but no one questioned us.

One Saturday evening I was sitting in the dim, smoky Mountain Room, laughing with my crowd, when a friend leaned across the table and said, "Joan, your mother just walked in." I whirled around and saw her in the doorway. I can still picture her there, huddled in a winter coat, just inside the room, gesturing to me. I quickly stubbed out my cigarette and hurried toward her. She seemed nervous and anxious to leave.

"Chief Timmons called the house and told Daddy there's going to be a raid," she said. "You'd better come with me. Go tell your friends, but hurry up."

I heard the next day that by the time the cops arrived, everybody under eighteen had fled.

Five years after that adventure, I had graduated from college and was living in Manhattan, working at an ad agency, and sharing an apartment in the East 20s with two other girls. I was dating a boy named Roy, whom I'd met through my former college roommate's boyfriend; they both worked at *Esquire* magazine. Roy and I had hit it off on our first date; he was tall, a reader, a music lover, and a graduate of Colgate, where he'd majored in English. He lived with three friends in an Upper West Side apartment with dark green living room walls and a door that opened onto the street.

When my father's troublemaking sister, Aunt Hazel, who had finally married and moved to New York City, learned that I had a serious boyfriend, she invited the two of us to her Washington Heights apartment for dinner. Her kindly but browbeaten husband, Uncle Victor, was there, and all I remember of the meal is an appetizer of artichokes

In Aunt Hazel's eyes, Roy had two serious flaws: first, he wasn't Jewish, and, as a result of polio he'd contracted when he was fourteen, he walked with a cane. This was such a natural element of his appearance that it didn't trouble me. But both of these characteristics impelled Aunt Hazel, for whatever reason, to embark on an all-out campaign to break up our romance.

She began bombarding me with phone calls and sending me alarming letters. At the same time, she was warning my parents about the terrible mistake I was making. I didn't realize then how much she'd upset them. I started hanging up on her phone calls and tearing up her letters, but I do remember two things she said: she asked why I didn't find a nice Jewish boy like Eddie Fisher, and she told me if I didn't end the relationship I would give my father a heart attack and my mother a nervous breakdown.

Roy and I had met in the summer; in November we decided to take the train to Tupper Lake to spend Thanksgiving weekend with my parents and two teenage sisters. We traveled overnight and pulled into the station the morning of Thanksgiving Day. When we stepped off the train my mother was standing on the platform, bundled in a heavy coat. I remember how cold it was, well below freezing.

After we arrived at the house, I could see that my parents were tense and upset, and I gradually realized that they had been driven almost out of their minds by my aunt's constant badgering. My mother managed to serve Thanksgiving dinner, but they both refused to drink the wine Roy had brought as a gift. Later, my mother spent an hour lying in her darkened bedroom, flattened by a migraine. My father left for my grandmother's house and didn't come back.

The next morning Roy and I decided it would be best for him to return to the city and for me to stay a little longer and try to work things out. As we walked down the front steps on our way to the station, my mother hurried out of the house carrying a package wrapped in brown paper and held it out to Roy. "Here are a couple of turkey sandwiches to eat on the train, dear," she said, "and a piece of pumpkin pie."

Roy and I were married the next August. His parents had not been happy about our impending wedding, either. His father, a high-school science teacher, was a remote, taciturn man. His mother, a librarian who considered herself a sophisticate, was a tall, busty woman who, unlike my own mother, smoked cigarettes and drank cocktails, which she served with hors d'oeuvres before dinner. Neither approved of Roy's choice of a small-town Jewish girl. Nonetheless, his mother agreed to arrange a reception on the terrace behind their Long Island house; my father sent her a check to cover the expenses.

I knew my mother and sisters would be at our wedding, but my father wouldn't make a commitment. At the last minute, though, he surprised us by showing up. We all gathered at eleven in the morning at a courthouse in Mineola, not far from Roy's parents' home. We were married by a judge wearing a grey gabardine suit and a striped tie with a grease stain in the center. My sisters and I tried to stifle fits of nervous giggles, while Roy's sentimental Uncle Gerrit, who'd driven down from Albany, brushed away his tears.

After the short ceremony, my father slipped the judge a twenty-dollar bill and we all went to lunch at Patricia Murphy's Candlelight Restaurant. I sat across the table from my mother, and I remember thinking how pretty she looked, her cheeks flushed from sips of champagne, as she smiled at Roy's father sitting next to her and managed to charm him into a conversation.

At my in-laws' house a crowd of our friends had gathered for the reception. To reach the terrace, where snacks, drinks, and the wedding cake had been set up, guests had to walk through the living room, which, just a few days before, had been freshened up with a coat of ivory paint. Of all the people there, it had to be my father, in his new brown suit, who brushed a sleeve against what was probably the only inch of paint that hadn't yet dried.

My mother asked for some turpentine and a piece of cloth, and calmly dabbed at his jacket. The other guests mingled on the terrace while my new mother-in-law fussed around my parents, biting her lip in annoyance. My father appears in that suit in a black-and-white photograph I have of Roy, me, and my family grouped on the lawn beyond the terrace. My mother is standing next to Roy. She's wearing a dark dress with a double row of buttons down the front and a little hat. She's smiling.

As I examine the picture now, I feel a wave of loyalty and sadness for both of my parents. I recognize the isolation of their lives in Tupper Lake, and their fears about the new, unknown world I was entering. Over the years they told me many times how sorry they were for the way they'd behaved toward Roy.

"He's such a fine young man," my mother often said, and my father seemed to agree.

Fifteen months after our wedding, our baby girl was born. We were living in Brooklyn Heights, in an apartment on the parlor floor of a brownstone on a leafy street. Roy and I slept in the high-ceilinged living room, on a bed that we covered during the day with an Indian-print spread; we'd set up the small bedroom for the baby.

The day we brought her home, my parents traveled down to the city to see their first grandchild and to help us out. They checked into a hotel a few blocks from our street. I remember two scenes from that first day. When I unbuttoned my sweater to nurse the baby, my father retreated into the kitchen in embarrassment, and wouldn't rejoin us until I was finished. Then Roy offered to make us some sandwiches. "You know how to cook?" my father said, amazed that a man was able to fix lunch.

I don't recall just what my mother was doing that afternoon. But in the middle of the night, when the baby had been crying for hours and Roy and I were frantic, we called her at the hotel. When I think of that night I can see her putting down the phone, telling my father she had to go, quickly slipping into her clothes and winter coat, and rushing alone down the dark Brooklyn streets.

Within minutes of our call, it seemed, she arrived at our apartment, shook off her coat, and held out her arms. After one last sob, the baby's eyes slowly closed and she fell peacefully asleep on my mother's shoulder.

When My Father Died

I was on the telephone in the kitchen, talking to my mother in California. The phone was mounted on the wall and had an extra-long cord, so I could move around the room during a conversation, stirring the soup, putting dirty pots in the sink. This was 1977, and I was living with my husband and four children in a big old house in a New York suburb.

My parents had moved to Santa Monica from Tupper Lake about twenty years before. My mother had taken a job with the telephone company, and worked her way up to become secretary to a vice president. My father, thirteen years older than she, had sold his baking business in upstate New York before the move. Since then, he seemed to have spent most of his time in his Barcalounger, reading or watching TV. But now he was in the hospital, very sick, maybe dying.

My mother wouldn't tell me the truth. She was never good at disclosing bad news; she kept it from us as long as she could. When she was diagnosed with breast cancer and had a mastectomy two years earlier, she didn't tell me about it until it was all over and she was back home.

She waited almost a week before she called to let me know my father was in the hospital. "Well, he has a few problems, and he's not a young man," she said. "There's the emphysema, and he's fallen a few times. The doctor calls them mini-strokes. Once he fell and hit his head on the nightstand and I had to call the paramedics. They got here in five minutes. Two very nice young men."

"I want to come and see him," I said.

"No, no, not now. Wait until your father leaves the hospital and comes home. Then you can come and visit and it will be much more pleasant."

But according to my sister Abby, who lived about an hour north of my parents, our father probably wouldn't be coming home. He was seventy-nine years old, one thing had led to another, and it didn't look good. I told Abby I'd be there the next day. I made a plane reservation and packed my bag.

My mother called that evening. Her voice was tense and I could feel her lips compressing every word. "Abby tells me you plan to come tomorrow. I wish you would put it off another few days. It's hard enough for me to handle this without another crying person here that I have to worry about. Your sister got so upset the last time she came to the hospital that I told her not to come back."

So I cancelled my reservation. She was so adamant; her tone was so harsh. The next morning she called again. This time her voice was muffled. "Daddy died last night," she said.

I took an early flight the next morning; the funeral was to take place that afternoon. My mother said he'd wanted to be cremated, but it was hard to imagine my parents even having that discussion.

My father wasn't religious. He'd told me that when he was young he went every Friday night and Saturday morning to services in the small wooden synagogue in Tupper Lake, but by the time he reached his twenties he realized he didn't believe any of it. Still, he and my mother always took my sisters and me to the synagogue on the high holidays. I remember looking across the room from my seat next to my mother and watching my father, a white prayer shawl around his shoulders, mumbling into a prayer book. When he glanced over and saw me, he winked.

His funeral service wasn't held in a synagogue, though, but in a bland funeral home. After my sister Linda and her husband, who'd driven down from San Jose, met me at the airport, we followed directions to a low white building on a corner in West Hollywood. My mother was there waiting for us, along with Abby and her family and a couple of other relatives. I don't remember how my mother greeted me, how she looked, or what she was wearing. But I still see, standing before this small group, a dark-suited rabbi who had never met my father speaking solemnly about what a good person he had been.

In truth, he was a complicated, often difficult man, detached from us children, sometimes sarcastic and hurtful to us and our mother. But not always. A frustrated artist turned businessman, he encouraged us to draw and paint, and I still remember dramatic stories he told us about his boyhood.

In his later years, he became increasingly isolated. My mother did everything for him, even coming home at noon to fix his lunch. He had lost the sight in one eye, so now when they went out my mother did the driving. She sometimes took him to a spot by a marina to look at the ocean. Although he was physically able to get around, they didn't go to restaurants or movies and she never introduced him to her friends.

After the short service, I walked outside alone. Behind the building was a lawn strewn with flat brass markers and pots of flowers. I have no idea if my father's ashes were buried there or if my mother took them. I couldn't bring myself to ask her, since I had learned when I was very young not to ask questions that might upset her. On my many visits to her after my father's death, we never returned to the spot where his ashes might, or might not, have been placed.

We all moved on to my mother's small, Spanish-style house and sat around the living room, reminiscing and laughing at old family stories as people tend to do after a death. My mother was sitting next to me on the couch, a photo album on her lap, smiling at snapshots of my sisters and me as children. Finally, gathering my courage, I turned to her and told her how sad I was that she hadn't given me a chance to see my father once more before he died, that he'd never known I had tried to be with him.

"I didn't want you to see him looking so sick," she said. "I wanted you to think of him the way he used to be."

I remember somebody telling me—of course it had to have been my mother—that shortly before he died my father said, "Where is Linda?" Even now, so many years later, I feel a stab of anguish that he didn't ask for me, and that I wasn't there.

I stayed with my mother for several more days, accompanying

her as she drove around Santa Monica, waiting while she took care of paperwork at various offices. We'd pick up something for dinner and share it at her kitchen table, chatting about the family, then we'd watch a little television, read for a while, and go to bed early. She seemed more tense than usual, and more subdued, but I never saw her cry.

In the middle of every night I was awakened by the sound of her heels clicking on the concrete path behind her house. I didn't get up; I just pictured her out there in the warm California darkness, pacing back and forth, back and forth.

Over the following months, my mother remade her life. She had retired from her job, and now that my father was gone, she was free to throw herself into volunteer work, go to concerts and movies with her friends, and meet them every day for walks along the ocean and meals in their favorite restaurants. I was happy that she was enjoying herself.

My mother had always been strong and independent. She preferred to take care of things herself, with no help. But that time, when she insisted on handling my father's death alone, she was wrong. And I never really forgave her.

Having Her Way

My mother was never satisfied with the first table she chose in a restaurant. When I visited her in California, we often ate out. She would take a seat, and whoever was with her—me, my husband, my sisters—would pick our chairs or slide into a booth. Then she'd look around the room and see a spot she liked better. Maybe it was near a window, or farther from the air conditioner's breeze, or it just had that indefinable something that caught her attention.

Once, on the patio of a Santa Monica restaurant where several of us had gathered for lunch, the only table that struck her as appropriate happened to have been chosen by other people, who were just opening their menus. My mother approached them. She was in her sixties then, a small, pleasant-looking woman. When confronting strangers with requests, she was polite but firm. She had an air of determination that people seemed unable to resist.

I watched my mother explain to the seated group that their space was the only one where our family could possibly sit; maybe it was shadier, or had more room. The rest of us stood back and saw the people rise from their chairs and take their menus to another table. I was more amused than embarrassed, and, looking back, I still admire her gumption.

Many of her displays of stubbornness took place when she was behind the wheel of her car, a '74 Chevy Monte Carlo, dark reddish-brown with a wide grille and long, curving fenders. After my father died she had moved to a small community just off the northbound lanes of the Pacific Coast Highway, which parallels the ocean. To get to Santa Monica, where she went several times a week, she had to drive south for a few miles. She could have turned north onto the highway and gone the short distance to Sunset Boulevard, where there was a traffic light. But no, she insisted on waiting for a break in the oncoming traffic, speeding across two lanes, and wedging the car into the southbound flow.

A few times when I happened to be with her during that maneuver, I clutched the armrest and gritted my teeth. "Mom," I'd say, "why don't you just go to Sunset and turn around at the light? This is so dangerous."

She'd tighten her lips and ignore me. As always, I was defenseless in the face of her tenacity.

Her home was a few miles from the Getty Museum, which had a collection of ancient artifacts and expansive gardens. You could reach the entrance from the highway, admission was free, and I thought it would be a perfect place for the two of us to spend an afternoon.

"No, I don't think so. You wouldn't like it," she said each time I suggested a visit. I didn't argue; I knew I'd lose. What did she have against the Getty Museum? I'll never know, and I never got to see it.

She was just as convincing when dealing with authority figures. Once she told me the story of her encounter with a police officer when she was driving to her volunteer job at Santa Monica Hospital. She was tooling along, almost there, when she saw a police car in back of her, its red lights flashing. She didn't stop until she arrived at the hospital's parking lot. The cop pulled in behind her, lights still twirling, and walked over to her window.

"Ma'am," he said, "do you realize you just drove through a red light?"

"Officer," she said, "I never drive through red lights."

He just shook his head and walked away.

In 1994, when she was eighty-four years old, she was still driving down to the hospital three days a week. That January, at four-thirty on a Wednesday morning, a strong earthquake struck Los Angeles. It was about eight o'clock in New York when a friend called and told me to turn on the television. Frantic newscasters appeared on the screen, predicting widespread damage, injuries, deaths.

Certain I wouldn't be able to reach my mother, but desperate to contact her, I dialed her number. After two rings I heard her say, "Hello," in her usual ladylike voice. The tremors had shaken her awake, she said, and she'd heard things falling off shelves, but it was too dark to see what had happened and her electricity was out.

I told her about the damage I'd seen on television and that Santa Monica had been especially hard hit. "I'm sure the Pacific Coast Highway won't be open," I said. "Don't even think of trying to get to the hospital today."

"We'll see," she said, her usual response when she was determined to do whatever she wanted.

A few hours later, my husband and I sat in front of the TV, drinking coffee and watching shots of collapsed houses, burning buildings, and crumbling roadways. We heard the announcer say that because of rockslides and rubble, the Pacific Coast Highway had been closed.

We were shown a helicopter shot of a length of the highway four lanes wide and completely empty of traffic. Then, at the top of the screen, a lone car appeared, traveling south. It moved purposefully along, all alone, until it drove out of sight.

"Look," said my husband, "there goes your mother."

Joan's mother and her first great-grandchild

47

My Mother's Cookies

On a Friday afternoon in late December I was in the kitchen of my New York apartment, standing at the stove stirring a fragrant pot of pork and red chili stew. My son was visiting with his three-year-old boy, Chris, and I was cooking one of their favorite meals.

The stew had been simmering for a couple of hours and I was about to start the rice when the telephone rang. I walked around the corner to the hall table and picked it up. A man's voice, a choked voice I didn't recognize, said, "Hello, Joan, this is Joe. Your mother, your mom, she passed away last night."

My mind stalled and I couldn't speak. It was my sister Abby's husband, on the phone from California: "We got a call from her neighbor. She hadn't shown up for her volunteer job at the hospital. They found her dead in her bed."

I turned to my husband. "My mother's dead," I sobbed. He took the phone from my hand. My son and grandson came in from the next room and stood side by side, looking at me, the little one clinging to his two faded flannel blankets. "I'm sorry, Mom," said my son.

What do you do next, when you find out your mother is dead? It was still dinnertime. The pork and chili stew was still bubbling on the stove. My family was still hungry. I wandered back into the kitchen and got the rice going, started heating the beans. Little Chris shuffled in, dragging the two blankets. He held one out to me. "Grandma," he said, "you can use this if you have to cry some more."

But I didn't cry anymore. After dinner I called Abby. "Just think about it," she said. "She wasn't sick, she didn't suffer. It's a blessing that she went peacefully in her sleep."

I didn't feel blessed. I wanted my mother. I needed to see her and talk to her just one more time. I was flooded with sadness at not spending every minute with her on my last trip to California, not paying enough attention to her, not listening carefully to her reminiscences.

That night I went to bed feeling heavy and stunned, but I slept soundly. In the early morning, in that otherworldly hour illuminated by a thin gray light, I saw my mother floating in space in a dark dress, on her face an expression of anguish.

When her face appears before me now, though, she is usually smiling and content, the way she looked when I visited her a month before she died. She had found me a place to stay, a small hotel in Santa Monica near a trendy promenade. I had wanted to spend my five-day visit at her neat, cozy home as I had in earlier years, but she discouraged me. "It's too boring in my little house," she said. "There are lots of interesting shops near the hotel. You'll enjoy it more."

I realized after her death that if I'd stayed with her I would have disrupted her carefully managed routine, and I would have been able to see the signs of her failing heart—the weakness and shortness of breath—that she had been so careful not to tell us about.

On my last day in California she invited us to lunch—Abby, Joe, and me. We helped her set up a table in the living room and carry in the sandwiches and salad she'd made. She laughed and joked with us and told favorite family stories. When it was time to go she packed a dozen of her special cookies into an empty candy box, nestling them in wax paper, chunky chocolate squares with a peanut butter filling and a thick fudgy frosting she had slicked on in little waves.

"You might get hungry in the evening," she said as she pressed the box into my hands and hugged me goodbye for the last time.

I meant to ask her for the cookie recipe. I still have the recipe, though, for the pork and chili stew I was making the day she died. It's in an old cookbook that I often use when company is coming. While I'm leafing through the stew section searching for an idea, I always stop at that page, consider it for a moment, and then move on.

Gifts

I was sitting with my sisters Abby and Linda on the floor of Abby's guest bedroom; we were surrounded by cardboard cartons and stuffed plastic bags. It was a few months after our mother's death. Since they lived the closest, Abby and her husband had driven down to clear out Mom's small house and have everything trucked up to their home in Ojai. I'd traveled from New York to help sort things out, and Linda had come from Morgan Hill, just south of San Jose.

Linda and I were looking through old photographs when Abby reached into a shoebox marked "Naturalizer Oxfords, size 6, tan" and pulled out a string of deep blue ceramic beads, enfolded in white tissue paper. She held them up to the light.

"I gave her these for Christmas, God knows how many years ago," she said. "I don't think she ever wore them."

Our mother had a problem with presents. Starting when we were children, she seemed to rarely use the gifts we gave her. At first we presented her with tiny bottles of Evening in Paris perfume and round, flowered boxes of dusting powder that we bought at Cohn's drugstore. As we grew older, we tried fancier things she might not buy for herself–nightgowns, satin bedroom slippers, silky bathrobes.

She'd tuck them in a dresser drawer, and months, even years, later, when one of us was visiting, she'd pull out something soft wrapped in tissue paper and say, "Why don't you take this, dear? It never really fit me properly."

My sisters and I usually accepted whatever she offered, even if we didn't really want it. Afterward we contemplated why it was so difficult for her to enjoy our gifts. Could it have been the result of her sad, lonely childhood when holidays weren't celebrated? Did she somehow feel she wasn't deserving? Whatever the reason, we kept on trying.

She loved to read; she always had books on her coffee table

and stacked by the side of her bed. With this in mind, one year for Christmas I ordered her a subscription to the *New Yorker*. She thanked me politely, but in our next phone conversation she said, "You know, I really don't care for magazines."

Once I had a houseplant delivered for her birthday. "Yes, dear, it got here right on time," she said when I called. "But it was a very strange-looking plant. I asked the florist to come pick it up and bring me something a little nicer."

I remember only two times when I gave her a gift she really liked. Once it was a blue Delft wall clock with a harbor and windmill design in the center and stylized flowers around the rim. She hung it over the table in her sunny kitchen, where we had our morning coffee when I visited.

The other was for her eighty-fourth birthday, when I made a contribution in her name to a charity called Women in Need. "What a wonderful idea," she said. "Something like this means so much more than anything you can buy in a store."

I don't know what happened to me at Christmas that same year. Once again, I had to choose a gift and get it in the mail on time, but I kept putting off making a decision. I remember that I didn't come across a Women in Need ad soliciting Christmas contributions, and I didn't take steps to find another charity. I ended up not buying her anything.

My family would be gathering in my apartment on Christmas Day, and I decided to call my mother then and have everyone talk to her; I hoped the call would make up for my negligence. By one in the afternoon we were all together: my two sons, two daughters, their husbands, and the four grandchildren. First I talked to my mother, then my husband said a few words, and one by one the others came to the phone to wish her a happy day. Only Rachel, a temperamental four-year-old, refused to talk. I was determined that every single person in the room had to speak to my mother.

I raised my voice. "Rachel," I said, "you must talk to your great-grandmother." My tone was so compelling that she stopped

51

pouting and came to the phone. Five days later my mother died.

The morning after her death, my sister Abby found on my mother's bedside table the book she'd been reading that night. The book, *The Kennedy Women*, had been a Christmas gift from my sister Linda. For a long time I tortured myself by thinking of my mother enjoying Linda's gift while I had given her only a phone call. Even something she didn't really care for would have been better than nothing at all.

The Things I Brought Home

I have only a vague memory of everything my sisters and I unpacked when we went through the things our mother had left behind, although I recall a surprising number of SAS Comfort shoes, the broad, flat-heeled kind that I vowed I would never wear. We each chose things we wanted to keep, and in the end I came away with very little.

A small enamel bowl from China sits on my desk. Its background is sky blue, and it's decorated with green leaves and red and yellow flowers. I wanted this bowl because my mother always kept it on her coffee table, and I thought it would remind me of her and her neat, comfortable living room. On my desk, though, it's just a bowl.

Atop a bookcase in my bedroom is a photograph of a woman attired in the style of the early 1900s. Her dress is cut high on the neck and the sleeves are snug, with puffs of material draped across the bodice and shoulders; the skirt curves out below a close-fitting waist. Her dark hair is gathered into soft waves and formed into a bun at the crown of her head. She is unsmiling. Her eyes look blue, like my mother's. I do not know who this woman is.

In a box in a dresser drawer I keep another of my mother's belongings—a silver ring, small enough to fit a child. A tiny diamond is set in its center, surrounded by delicate filigree. I had never seen this ring before I found it wrapped in tissue paper and tucked into a box of my mother's keepsakes. Sometimes I wear it on my little finger.

Other things that I carried home bring her more to life for me. In a large manila envelope, I keep a few dozen photographs she had saved. Along with pictures of her children and grandchildren, there are several that show her life in California—posing with a group of friends in a Santa Monica park, striding along the promenade that parallels the ocean. In another, wearing a trim grey suit with white collar and cuffs, she stands next to her boss at the telephone company, Mr. Snodgrass. She kept a letter from him dated June 1974, a time when she was recovering from a mastectomy and deciding to retire from her job as his secretary.

"I sincerely hope your recovery is completely satisfactory," Mr. Snodgrass wrote. "It was always such a real pleasure to work and talk with you... I miss you at that desk."

I can see my mother the way she must have appeared to him—a petite woman, always neatly dressed, pleasant and efficient. I like knowing that he was fond of her.

After she retired, she became a volunteer at Santa Monica Hospital, and I have the nametag she wore. When I look at it I remember stories she told of times she guided movie stars toward their doctors' offices, and brought updates on patients having surgery to waiting families. The laminated plastic tag has her photo in one corner; she is smiling, and I can see the collar of the rose-colored jacket she wore as a volunteer. The day after she died, when Abby was called to her house, she saw the jacket on the closet door where my mother had hung it, ready to be slipped on in the morning.

In Her Secret Life

"Yes," is the first thing my mother says, "I was quite a cute little girl." Hearing her voice again, so warm and melodious, is as painful as I'd feared.

It's 1995, several months after my mother's death in California, and I'm sitting at my desk at home in New York. I've just begun listening to an audiotape that I kept in a small cardboard box tucked into a drawer, a Fuji tape, sixty minutes long, with a white stick-on label marked "Mom–1976."

My sister Linda made this tape–an interview with our mother– for an adult education course in women's issues she was taking at a community college in northern California. I'd known about it for almost twenty years, but never asked for a copy. Since childhood I'd sensed that my mother was keeping painful secrets; I suspected these secrets would be revealed on the tape, and I couldn't bear to face them. But after her death I asked Linda to mail me the tape; even then it was months before I could play it.

As I hear my mother's opening words, I realize she and Linda must have been looking at a photograph that I now have, the only one that shows my mother before I was born. She appears to be twelve or thirteen, and is standing next to her father in front of a wooden building. Her head is turned slightly to the side and she's smiling. Her glossy black hair is pulled back with a ribbon, and she's wearing a loose, light-colored dress, dark stockings, and laced-up leather boots. Her father, a stocky man with thick dark hair, formally dressed in a three-piece suit, looks serious but kindly.

My mother was born Shirley Jean Wallock in 1910 in Cohoes, a mill town in upstate New York. Her parents, Joseph and Anna Wallock, had settled there after emigrating from Russia in 1900. Together they ran a general store. They eventually had six children; my mother was their fourth.

"I remember my poor mother," says my own mother on the

tape. "She was a frail woman, and with all those children... My father wasn't home. He went away to cure."

Diagnosed with tuberculosis, her father had moved to Tupper Lake, a small village in the northern Adirondacks; it was thought the fresh, pine-scented air could cure the illness. The rest of the family stayed in Cohoes, where her mother ran the store until she died in the flu epidemic of 1918. After her death, says my mother, "My father didn't know what to do with us. He couldn't cope with us."

The three oldest children joined their father in Tupper Lake, the two youngest were adopted, and my mother, only eight years old, was sent first to an orphanage, then to live with an uncle and aunt in Cohoes.

The aunt, says my mother on the tape, "was a mean woman, like a wicked witch... She had a daughter who was retarded. I had the care of this girl. She was my responsibility."

When I hear this I remember myself as a child, sitting on the toilet seat lid in our pale green bathroom while my mother brushed my straight brown hair and braided it into pigtails. I remember the feeling of my forehead resting against her soft belly while I breathed in the laundry scent of her cotton housedress.

As she fastened my braids with rubber bands she began talking about little girls and hairstyles and I was only half listening. Then she said, "I was living in a house where there was a girl who sat on the floor all day rocking back and forth and blowing on a silver teaspoon." Why the girl was doing this was a mystery to me, but I didn't ask my mother. Yet so many years later I still recall the image I had then of the girl and the spoon.

My mother was eventually sent to live with a childless couple in Detroit, and stayed with these strangers for four years, sometimes traveling to Tupper Lake to visit her father. "I went back and forth, took the train all by myself, this little kid," she says. She slept overnight on the train and the conductor took care of her. "He woke me up in the morning so I could see Niagara Falls."

When she was fifteen she returned to live with her father for good, sharing an apartment over the store where he sold sewing machines and musical instruments. "I was very thin," she says, "and they worried about me. So the doctor in Detroit said, 'She's lonely for her father.' I didn't really know my father that well. I was just lonely for a normal, happy life, I guess. And then..." She pauses. "Did I ever tell you that my father took his own life?"

One day she came home from school and walked upstairs. Her father's bedroom door was closed and locked from the inside with a hook. "I rapped and knocked and pounded and nobody answered," she says. She ran to get something to jab at the hook until it gave way. "I pushed the door open and I found him dead on the floor. Hung himself."

I have a copy of a document from Surrogate's Court, Franklin County, the county where her father died. It is a petition from an Isaac Bloomberg, described as "friend and creditor" of Joseph Wallock, who "departed this life" on the ninth of September, 1925. He left no will, the document states, and the property he possessed "is estimated to be of the value of $200."

Those entitled to his estate are listed as Esther, Isadore, and Sadie Wallock. Esther was my mother's older sister; she later settled in Brooklyn, never married, worked in a dress shop, and visited us once a year. Isadore—who had changed his name to Irving by the time I knew him—was her older brother. Sadie had to have been my mother; I'd thought her name had always been Shirley. There's no mention of the two youngest children, a girl and a boy, who had been adopted by strangers.

There's no mention, either, of the oldest boy, Max, and when I was a child my mother never talked about him. But one day he paid us a surprise visit. I was playing paper dolls with my sisters on the living room rug when someone knocked at the front door. I can still see the man who stood there—a bulky, smiling person with gifts in his hands. I remember the present he gave me: a shiny wooden box with a colorful picture of a snow-capped mountain on the lid.

Inside the box were neat stacks of writing paper and envelopes, tied with narrow ribbons. I thought it was wonderful.

I recall my mother standing, talking to the man, and my father appearing. There was more talk, and then the man was gone. She must have told me that he was her brother Max, but I don't know how she explained his sudden appearance and abrupt departure. I could tell she was nervous, my father upset, and something was wrong that I didn't understand. We never saw him again.

"I guess he wrote to me after he left," my mother says on the tape, recounting the visit. But my father never showed her the letters, she says. He tore them up. "Max was trouble," she says. "He was always trouble. When he was a young boy he was hit by a streetcar and had stitches in his head. I don't think he was ever right after that."

One day several years after Max's visit, another stranger appeared. I heard a knock at the door and opened it to see a tall, well-dressed, grey-haired man. He asked for my mother. She greeted him warily and led him to the living room. I leaned against the wall around the corner, close enough to listen.

He told my mother he had found out where she lived and traveled from his home on Long Island. He said he and his wife had adopted her baby sister, Mollie; they called her Mildred. They had never told her she was adopted, but he was getting old and had been ill; he wondered if they should tell her now.

"He asked me what I thought he should do," says my mother on the tape. "I said, 'I don't know what kind of temperament she has. It would be a terrible shock to her. It might not be a good idea. But I'd like to have a picture of her if you have one.'"

I don't know if my mother told me at the time how upsetting this was, how much she wanted to see her sister again, or if I heard her telling my father. But I could see she was troubled for days after the visit.

Then an envelope arrived in the mail. There was no return

address, no note inside, only a small black-and-white photograph. I have the picture now; I found it among my mother's papers after she died. It shows a smiling, dark-haired young woman sitting on a couch, a chubby baby in her lap.

This cheerful-looking woman was two years old the last time my mother had seen her. Her youngest sibling, Frankie, was an infant. "I have no idea where he is," she says on the tape. "He could be living right down the street."

I last saw my mother when I visited her for a few days a month before she died. One day she drove me to Marina del Rey and parked near the walkway that runs along the ocean. We sat in the car enjoying the salty air and chatting about the array of people passing by. Then she took a breath and started to tell me a story. I don't remember her words, but somehow I knew she was going to recall a painful incident, one of the secrets she'd kept hidden for so long. Something in me resisted; I interrupted her, switched to a different subject.

Now, so many years after her death, I picture us sitting in that car again, the ocean breeze drifting through the open windows. This time I listen while she tells me about her past, stories I heard later, on the tape. This time I ask the right questions: What was it like to have your mother die, to find your father's body on the floor, to live with strangers, to lose your little sister and brother?

She tells me everything I need to know. Then we get out of the car and stroll along the walkway, enjoying the sun and the splashing of the surf. She's smiling and we're both happy, looking forward to our day together, deciding which restaurant to choose for lunch.

Joan's mother with her father, Joseph Wallock

Ashes

My sister Abby carried my mother's ashes from the funeral home in Santa Monica to her house in Ojai. She took them with her when she moved to Grass Valley in northern California, and then to her next home in Mesquite, Nevada, a town near the Utah border. The ashes were in a brown cloth bag she never opened.

My two sisters and I had begun disagreeing the day after our mother died. Since I was in New York, Abby and Joe made arrangements for the cremation. I wanted to fly out to California and scatter the ashes from a walkway along the ocean in Marina del Rey, a spot that my mother loved and where she had taken me on my last visit. Linda said no, we'd have to get permission, what if someone saw us, and anyhow she couldn't bear to see what the bag contained.

The next day Abby called to tell me she'd heard from a chaplain at Santa Monica Hospital, where our mother had volunteered for so many years. Because of her devotion to her job and her popularity among the staff, the chaplain wanted to hold a memorial service for our mother in the hospital's chapel. I told Abby I thought that was a wonderful idea. But Abby said no, she didn't want people offering her their condolences, didn't want her tears to be on display. She was adamant and, to my later regret, I gave in.

There was no memorial service, no spreading of ashes, only the bag of my mother's remains that Abby carried from house to house each time she moved. When she was living in Grass Valley, she thought of planting a lilac bush—our mother's favorite flower—in front of her house and burying the ashes beside it. But she soon decided she didn't care for the climate in Grass Valley, so she and Joe packed up and moved to the Nevada desert.

My mother didn't leave any last wishes. She wouldn't talk about dying. Once on a visit, over lunch in a cafe, I told her Roy and I had

61

recently signed a living will that our lawyer prepared. She didn't take the bait, just looked away and changed the subject.

By then, when she was in her eighties, many of her friends were gone. Death and loss were on her mind, as I discovered when I read a slip of paper that Abby had found tucked into a pocket sewn to the arm of Mom's reading chair. In her distinctive blocky handwriting, she had copied a paragraph she must have found in a book:

"What must it feel like, to be her age, so very near the other end of herself, watching everyone she knew and loved go one by one through a door that was even now half-opened to her? What did she think came next? I knew she was not a conventionally religious woman, but I did not, I realized, know what she did think about life and death and what lay ahead."

It broke my heart to read those words. I pictured my mother sitting alone in her living room, an open book by her side and a pad of white paper in her lap, writing out this passage. So she did, of course, think about death. She just wouldn't talk about it, not to her daughters, in any case.

In April 2002, more than seven years after our mother's death, I suggested to my sisters that the three of us get together for a few days. We made a plan to stay at Abby and Joe's house in Mesquite, and, while we were there, to finally decide what to do about the ashes.

The first couple of days we lounged around, took walks, and ate buffet lunches at one of Mesquite's casinos. Joe told us he'd found a spot that he thought would be just right for spreading Mom's ashes. On the last day of my visit, he took us there. He drove out of town on a road that followed a gorge through looming rock walls and then into a strip of Arizona between the Nevada and Utah borders. He pulled off at an exit marked Cedar Pocket, steered the car up a short dirt road into a deserted recreation area, and parked.

My sisters and I climbed to a ridge that overlooked red and gold cliffs and scrubby desert plants poking out of the sand. Abby opened the bag and, taking turns, we scooped out handfuls of ashes and tossed them over the edge. The day was breezy, and bits of ash flew back toward us, settling on our faces and clothing.

As we walked back to the car where Joe was waiting, Abby and Linda said they thought the return of the ashes was eerie, that it was a signal from our mother. I knew it was just the wind.

Brooklyn

I placed my cursor on the Google space and typed my father's name: "Jesse Propp." I had been researching my mother's family for weeks, looking for information about the lives of her parents and siblings. It was fourteen years after her death and thirty-three years after my father's. But I had been ignoring my father. My story was not about him.

Then one morning I had a sudden urge to enter his name. It appeared in a second, in a link to a site that surprised me: bklyn-genealogy.info. I got that sick, scared feeling that comes when you're afraid you're going to learn something you didn't want to know.

I clicked on the link and was led to a long list of couples who'd been married in Brooklyn in 1931. Holding my breath, I entered my father's name and hit Enter. Up he popped under the heading 6 October 1931: Jesse Propp, 34, Tupper Lake, New York. And beneath it: Shirley Wallock, 21, 1751 Union Street. I finally learned, to my amazement, that my parents were married in Brooklyn. And not only that, my mother was living there, not in Manhattan, as I'd always assumed.

My mother and father never celebrated their anniversary, or even mentioned it. I never saw a photograph of their wedding. I didn't know where it was held or who was there. And I don't remember ever asking.

After my mother died and I began exploring her life, I tried to picture the wedding. I thought they might have been married in Tupper Lake's small wooden synagogue, standing before a grey-bearded rabbi, the pews filled with women in veiled hats and crinkly taffeta dresses and men with white prayer shawls draped over their dark suits.

But that didn't seem right. It was easier to envision them in a hurried ceremony in the stuffy parlor of a justice of the peace in some nearby village, with my father's LaSalle parked out front, ready to take them to a dim room in the local hotel. Because no joyous family or friends were moved to take a wedding picture, I could only believe it was a clandestine affair, not an event to be celebrated.

When we were young, my little sisters and I sometimes asked my parents how they met. "I was driving along in my car," said our father, "and I saw a girl walking along a dusty road." He stopped to pick her up, he said, and she turned out to be our mother. We loved the dusty road story, and often asked to hear it again. In my mind I saw the back of a small, slender young woman, wearing a faded cotton dress, walking along as puffs of dust swirled around her feet.

The truth was, my mother said many years later, that she met my father in August 1931 when she and her sister were visiting a friend in Tupper Lake. One day, after a picnic in a campground outside of town, they were caught in a rainstorm while waiting for the friend's father to pick them up. Along came Jesse Propp in his big black LaSalle. He stopped the car and they all piled in.

"I got in the back seat," my mother said. "I wasn't paying any attention to him. He was an older man."

That evening, he called the friend's house and asked to talk to her. "He wanted to take me out," my mother said. "That was the end of August and we got married the first of October." Actually, according to the Brooklyn records, they were married on October sixth. Had she forgotten the date?

After their marriage and move to Tupper Lake, they went out a few times, she said, usually for dinner and dancing at the country club. But my father had been around—he'd lived in Florida and Los Angeles, he'd run a dance hall in Tupper Lake—and now he was ready to settle down. He wasn't interested in going out to have fun.

"We were not compatible at all, really," my mother said. "I always felt sorry for him because I think he got a raw deal. He should have married somebody who made him happier."

She didn't mention her own unhappiness, but when I was growing up I could feel it. It wasn't only my father's often sarcastic, hurtful remarks, but her loneliness. She never said her husband made her happy, only her children. "I loved the children so much," she said. "They were a chance for me to have someone to love me, and for me to love."

I have no idea why she married my father so quickly. When she told the story of their short courtship, she never said he was charming, handsome, intelligent, that she fell in love with him instantly. But not long after my father died, after forty-five years of silence on the subject, she reflected on her decision.

"It wasn't very smart," she said. "He didn't know me and I didn't know him. I was really too young for him. But he was maybe sort of a father figure to me."

In the end, she looked back on her marriage with regret. Maybe that's why there were no anniversary celebrations, no framed photos of the happy couple. Maybe that's why, when I told her Roy and I were moving to Brooklyn, she didn't say, "Did you know that Dad and I were married in Brooklyn? And, as a matter of fact, that I was living in Brooklyn then? I still remember the address—1751 Union Street."

I'm at my computer again; I just want to take one more look at that Brooklyn wedding site. Once again I type "Jesse Propp" and hit Enter. This time a link appears that wasn't there before, and I'm led to the front page of *The Journal and Republican*, Lowville, New York, February 26, 1931. Squinting at the tiny type, I learn that Jesse Propp, Tupper Lake, was one of eighty-five people indicted for prohibition violations by the federal grand jury in Albany.

So my father was a bootlegger. He was indicted eight months before he married my mother. I wonder if he had to serve time in jail or just pay a fine. I wonder if he told my mother about this during their courtship. If he did, maybe it made him more dashing in her eyes. I dimly recall my mother joking, when I was just a kid, about my father smuggling something over the Canadian border. In my imagination, it was my mother that he was smuggling.

Vicki

Vicki and her mother, Patricia Boyle Malits

Getting There

As a child I was quiet and moody, and I stuck close by my mother, often frustrating her with my shyness and inhibitions. Yet there were times when I sensed her loneliness, and recognized the comfort my need brought her.

An avid reader, I started writing my own stories as soon as I could string words into sentences. Those narratives were imitations of the exotic lands and fascinating characters I discovered through books. Then, at thirteen, I began a journal, and soon I was filling notebook after notebook with my rambles. Interwoven with my daily musings were fragments of fiction, ideas I promised myself I'd come back to one day. At college, afraid to bring my writing into the open, I opted for a major in art history. I sat in darkened lecture halls, looking at slides of paintings and sculpture, thinking about stories I wanted to write.

It was during this time that the depression and anxiety cycling in and out of my life became constant companions. Going to classes took tremendous effort. Often I would creep through my days without speaking to or even looking at anyone else. I tried to be invisible. I hid in my room whenever possible. But I grew tired of being alone. During my teens I'd experimented with drinking and drugs, and now that behavior increased. When I was high, I was relaxed, I was outgoing, I was better. I put distance between my mother and me, afraid she'd realize how messed up I was, and that she'd be hurt or disgusted. Often, my guilt over having abandoned her haunted me.

With the help of good friends, I attained a fragile balance, stopping short of doing myself harm. I managed to finish school and find work. After the birth of the first of my two sons, I made the transition from party girl to wife and mother. I left my full-time career in museum education for part-time jobs. I still continued my journal, toyed with the beginnings of stories, but remained a closet writer. Through it all, my mother and I played tug-of-war, alternately struggling to hang onto and pull away from each other. At times I resented her, blaming her for my inadequacies, for teaching me to need her. Sometimes she was the only one with whom I could feel safe.

By now, my journal had become a necessity. I wondered about snipping out parts and teasing them into whole new worlds: fiction as a rearrangement of events and personalities. I also began to see the beauty, the stark beauty, of the simple facts of my life.

Then my mother got sick. In a year she was gone.

That was the spring of 1997. The shock and sorrow I felt at her passing was a catalyst. As I grieved, I grew determined not to fall into depression. If my mother had taught me anything by her life's example, it was resilience—to fight through the difficult times and find a way to be happy. I sought help for my mood disorders, realizing I no longer needed to struggle in shame or solitude. I began to take my writing seriously.

And so, a year after my mother's death, I enrolled in a writing workshop. At the first class, I sat at a large square table with several other women in the wood-paneled interior of a renovated train station that was home to a writers' center, listening as Joan introduced herself. Then each of us spoke briefly about our backgrounds.

I talked about my journal, how I had written stories as a child, how I'd always needed to write. I found myself telling these people I'd just met that my mother was gone and I wanted to write about her.

Joan asked us to write for fifteen minutes. I wrote about being in my mother's bedroom one evening when I was a little girl. My sister and I were putting makeup on our mother's face and rearranging her hair. But the writing I ended up doing in that workshop didn't just focus on my mother. The stories I wrote were scattered; they wandered through time and place.

It wasn't until years later, in our small writers group, that I found my way back to her.

Mommy

The grass is taller than I am, and it is golden and swaying under the noonday sun. I run with other children I do not know along the dirt path between these soft, dancing walls to the log cabin up ahead. Hot and so sunny that when I reach up to touch the top of my head, my dark hair cooks the palm of my hand. I am sweaty and dirty and very happy.

I climb the big steps to the front porch of the cabin, following the older girls and boys, and run through a forest of long, grown-up legs until I find the open doorway. I stop and then walk inside. My eyes take time to adjust to the dusk of indoors, and I stand where I am, unable to see for a moment. Then I hear my mother's laughter, loud and strong.

"Mommy!" I scream into the dark room. "Mommy!" I scream once more, and then she is there.

"What happened? What's the matter?" she asks as she kneels down, putting the beer can on the floor and her hands on my shoulders. She looks me up and down, inspecting me for injury, and then hugs me close to her.

"Are you okay?"

"Yes," I answer.

Springtime, and I am four years old. My mother and father stand at the other end of the yard, talking, a big bag of grass seed on the ground between them. I hear their voices but don't listen to their words. They are there but I am by myself. The dirt beneath me is chocolate brown, chunky and grooved, and the sun is directly overhead. I sink my shovel into the earth and it crunches. My left leg bends slightly at the knee as I lean all my weight down on the shovel. Up comes a wedge of soil. I lift and toss the shovelful over my right shoulder, then bend to peer into my new hole. The tail end of a worm flaps from one flattened side. I drop my shovel and scratch away at the earth with my dirt-blackened fingernails. Then I pull him out, careful not to rip him in two, and place him into the shoebox with my other pets. Already I have four or five soiled, blood-red earthworms, long and plump, wiggling their way down into the few inches of dirt that is their new home.

"I got lots of pets now!" I yell.

"Remember to put some little leaves and twigs in for food," Mom says.

Yes, I should feed them. But first I'll dig for a few more. Up off my knees, right foot planted firmly on the ground, I lean into my shovel once more. But I stop, look down at the place on my thigh where I feel a tickle. Rust-colored, winged, long bent legs crawling, the bug moves down my leg. My red shorts are wrinkled and bunched up in my crotch, and my white ankle socks and rubber-toed Keds are covered in dirt.

I freeze. I watch it move, I see each of its bent legs taking turns as it makes its way over my knobby knee. I feel the tickle, shy and teasing, but I anticipate its sting with terror.

"Mommy! Mommy!" I scream.

"What?" she says as she looks over at me, and then, "What's the matter?"

"A bee!" I tell her quietly now, afraid to make any noise, afraid to flinch.

She moves closer. She is wearing a pink blouse and plaid Bermuda shorts. She is barefoot. Her legs are fair and freckled. As she walks toward me, I see her toes sink into the soft earth and the footprints she leaves behind.

She moves gracefully, like a ballerina, lifting her right leg slowly, extending her foot, and with the lightest touch of her toe she flicks the bug from my knee, and it flies high and away. "It was a wasp," she tells me.

My mother has given me a new word.

"So, how are your pets doing?" she asks, bending to look into the shoebox.

"Wasp," I say to myself quietly, so I will remember, and I look down at the top of my mother's head.

I kneel on the vinyl padding of the kitchen chair that I have dragged over to the sink. My mother is washing dishes and I am watching. I like to be near her. Her hands are soapy; she scrubs hardened egg yolk from a dish with a yellow sponge. I put one hand into the warm water that fills the sink and scoop out some fuzzy soap bubbles. Then I hear the squeaking again.

"Hear it?" I say.

"I can't hear, the water is running. Wait," she says.

I climb down from the chair while my mother finishes the dishes. I sit on the floor and listen. Nothing for a few moments, then I hear it again. A faint squeaking. I look around. I try to figure out where it's coming from.

"You heard it again?" My mother is squatting next to me now, her head cocked to one side. "Maybe it's a bird."

We are both keeping very still. I hold my breath as long as I can, because if I don't breathe I can hear better. Nothing.

"Let's get you dressed," my mother says, standing and walking away. "It looks like it may rain soon. I want to get you kids outside while it's still nice."

I stay where I am, listening. I can hear my mother in the other room, talking to my brother and sister, but I am waiting for the squeaking sound. I hear it; it is coming from the broom closet. I crawl over to the door; it is open just a crack so I pull it open some more. I see it right away–a mouse. The head and two front legs of a tiny, gray mouse. The rest of it is inside a shiny metal box.

"Mommy! Mommy! I found it," I yell.

She comes running back into the kitchen, Debi in her arms and Eddie toddling behind her as fast as he can. She looks down and sees it. "Holy shit!" She plops Debi down next to me. "Watch your sister," she says, and then she gets down on the floor and peers in at the mouse.

Eddie tries to climb on her back.

"Holy shit, it's stuck. Goddamn it, stupid goddamn mousetrap."

Then she's up and the metal box is in her hands. She has a finger underneath the mouse's little chest, supporting him as he dangles from the round opening in the side of the box.

"Wait here," she says as she walks down the hallway.

I hear her voice from the bathroom.

"Oh my God, you poor thing. Goddamn it! Goddamn it!"

Then she's headed back to the kitchen.

"The stupid trap didn't work right," she's saying. "The poor mouse got stuck half in and half out. The trap door snapped down on its back."

This is the mouse that has been living with us for a week or more now. We'd see it scamper along the woodwork in the evenings while we sat in the living room watching TV. And in the morning while we ate breakfast it would hurry back to its hiding place under the refrigerator, running right across the middle of the kitchen floor, and Daddy would jump up and try to stomp on it with his big, black shoes. But it was too fast. Mommy would scream at Daddy not to crush it and Daddy would curse as he sat back down to breakfast. Mommy had taken us with her to the hardware store to buy the trap; it was the kind that was supposed to catch the mouse alive.

"There's no reason to kill the thing," she told Daddy.

Now she was looking in the refrigerator. I see her take out a piece of cheese. Then she picks Debi up off the floor and says, "Follow me."

I take Eddie's hand and we walk to the bathroom behind her.

The mouse is in the claw-footed bathtub, its ears and nose twitching as it drags its hindquarters around with its two good front legs.

"The trap crushed him in the middle. I don't think he can use his back legs anymore," Mommy says as she breaks off small pieces of cheese and places them in front of the mouse.

"Are we going to keep him?" I ask.

"I don't know what we're going to do," she says.

We watch the mouse nibble at the cheese. Eddie is trying to climb into the bathtub. Debi sits on the floor chewing on her fist.

We don't take baths that night. And later, lying in bed falling asleep, I hear Daddy come in from work and then he and Mommy are yelling about the mouse.

"You will not flush it down the toilet, you mean shit!" Mommy says.

I am hoping the mouse will get better and we can keep him forever.

The next morning, after breakfast, and after Daddy leaves for work, I follow my mother to the bathroom. Debi is napping in her crib and Eddie is in the playpen in the kitchen. I watch her take the mouse out of the bathtub and put him into a small brown paper bag.

"What are you doing?" I ask.

"It's okay, don't worry. I'm going to bring it to its new home."

She walks down the hallway to the kitchen.

Turning to me as she pushes the back door open she says, "Stay here with your brother. I'll be right back."

But I don't stay. I follow her out the door and into the yard. It is chilly. The wind is blowing and leaves are swirling all around, but the sky is like blue glass.

My mother walks quickly to the side of the yard and steps over the low wire fence that separates the property from the apartment building next door. Then she gets on her knees next to the cellar window of the building and opens the end of the paper bag, letting the mouse fall out. She pushes on the window and pokes the mouse until it crawls inside the cellar.

She stands and turns around, seeing me watching her.

"Daddy wouldn't let me keep it. But it will be safe inside the building. Warm. And it will find garbage to eat," she tells me.

I believe her. The mouse is going to be okay.

Outside of Her

It was spring 1964, and my mother was smoking her Winstons even as her belly swelled.

"You're going to have a baby brother," she told me one night. She sat on my bed and I sipped from the glass of water she had brought me. I was seven, and already had a little brother and a little sister. In our dark bedroom, in beds nearby, they slept, while I learned about the baby growing inside my mother. She was so sure it was a boy, even though she had no proof.

"Go to sleep," she said and left me. I put my head down on the pillow, trying to imagine the baby that would be here in the summer. It would be like a doll, small enough for me to hold, and I could give it a bottle. Then I called out to my mother again, telling her that I was still thirsty, but all I really wanted was for her to sit by my side once more.

That spring my mother and I would stand on the corner waiting for the school bus in the cool newness of those mornings, and I'd hold her hand as she chatted with other mothers. I'd hear her talk about feeling as big as a house. Her belly was like a beach ball being blown up in slow motion.

One afternoon I came home from school feeling nauseous, and that night I leaned over the side of my bed and vomited into a blue plastic trash bucket, as my mother rubbed my back. Between bouts of nausea, I'd lie back on my pillow and try to sleep. My mother stayed, curled up on the bottom of my bed. I had a fever, and felt I was floating in a dark cloud, unable to see, and I asked my mother, "Am I dead?"

Her cool hand touched my forehead as she said, "No, baby, you are sick. You have a virus. I'm here with you."

The next afternoon Dr. Billo came to the house, and while he watched the blood and bile pour into the bucket as I threw up, he told my mother I was dehydrated and needed to be in the hospital.

My mother held me down on the hospital bed as the nurses

struggled to strap my arms to the bars on each side and insert the IV needle. She left me there at night, and I cried quietly so the nurses wouldn't scold me for waking the other children. In the afternoons she came back and sat at my bedside, reading to me, showing me storybook pictures of butterflies and bluebirds. Her voice was hoarse, and her face looked loose and tired. I was there for three days.

After the hospital stay, the morning I was returning to school, I ate my breakfast and then vomited cereal and milk onto our kitchen floor. My mother, in one smooth movement, got up from her chair, came over to me, swung back her arm, and slapped her hand hard against my cheek.

"Do that again and you'll be right back in the hospital," she said.

I didn't cry, although the sting of the slap made my eyes water. In the past, whenever I'd misbehaved, I might have gotten a quick pat on my bottom, but this she had never done. I stood there and watched as she cleaned up the mess I had made. I felt as if my insides were shaking, as if I were full of insects crawling under my skin and onto my muscles. I looked at her back as she squatted in front of me mopping the floor with paper towels and I wanted to hit her. Instead, I waited until she finished and then I went upstairs to the bathroom to brush my teeth.

Later, at school, Sister Mary Eleanor hugged me when I walked into my first-grade classroom. She was sweet, young, and soft-spoken. Because of her I was able to bear the long hours away from home. As she held me close against the black robe of her habit, stroking my long brown hair, she said, "The class was praying for you to get better."

That afternoon my mother was waiting on the corner, as always. She smiled as she took my hand and I hopped off the bottom step of the school bus.

"I thought I heard the ice cream truck bells ringing. Let's wait and see if he comes round the corner," she said.

My brother and sister were sitting nearby on a patch of grass blotted yellow with dandelions. It was warm and I felt sleepy, and I leaned against my mother's side while we listened to the ringing of the bells getting closer. I didn't want any ice cream, but I knew I would pick the vanilla covered with the chocolate coating. I would eat it to make her happy.

On those spring nights, before my bedtime, when my father was at work and the house was still and dark, she and I would lie next to each other on her bed, the TV playing, the bedside lamp aglow. She smoked her Winstons, and sometimes blew smoke rings for me. If the telephone rang it would be her sister, and they would talk while I put my hand on her belly and felt the movement within.

Once, she pulled her shirt up over her stomach and I saw the porcelain skin, shiny and taut. The bulge rippled and shifted as the baby moved.

"Put your ear on my belly. Listen," she said.

I closed my eyes, resting my head on top of her stomach, and I heard the rumbles and whooshes, sounds like a tiny ocean trapped beneath her flesh.

"I remember when you were in there," she said.

Spring let go and summer came, the sun burning hot, bees buzzing, and the days long. My mother moved slowly, her heavy stomach hanging low. Then she was gone for almost a week. My father went to work and visited at the hospital, and my grandmother watched over my brother, sister, and me. I wouldn't eat, and let myself get used to the empty feeling inside me. Each day I stayed in my bed all morning. In the afternoon I sat next to my grandmother on the sofa, watching her soap operas, waiting for my mother to come back.

The day she came home I was standing in front of our house with my grandmother, and I watched my father park the big green Ford at the curb. He got out of the car and came around to open the door for my mother. He held her elbow as he helped her out of her seat. In her arms she held the baby, wrapped in a white and pink blanket.

I didn't move at first, just looked at my mother. When she smiled at me, so clean and pretty, I ran to her.

"Careful," she said as I wrapped my arms around her waist, and as she pulled away from me she leaned down to show me the baby.

"Here's your new sister," she said.

I didn't care. I didn't even look.

Snowstorm

We are separated by the glass of the storm door. I watch my mother on the other side. Snow is falling, heavy and white, and she shovels the walkway, clearing a path to our house. I hear the crunch of the snow and scrape of the shovel as she plunges it into the drifts and digs down to the concrete. Rhythmically, she pushes through the snow, lifting heaps and tossing it off to the side. I see the top of her head in a black woolen cap, and the fog she breathes out floating up and around her like a halo. I am sitting on the floor, still in my pajamas, wrapped in an afghan of red and green yarn my mother crocheted. I sniffle and cough. Eight years old, bored and angry; I want to play in the snow.

I push against the door to open it a crack. The frigid air rushes in and I shiver.

"Please!" I yell out to her.

"I told you no, and I am not going to answer you anymore," she says.

I have missed the last two days of school because of my cold. But today is a snow day and all the kids are staying home. My brother and sister are out in the backyard with our friends, bundled up in their snow pants, boots, jackets, scarves, mittens, and hats. When I crack the door open again I hear loud screams of laughter blowing around the side of the house with the snow. I let the door slam shut.

She doesn't look up. She is working fast, for she is getting cold and the path to the door is long. Behind her I see the evidence of her hard work disappearing; the snow doesn't quit, piling up as quickly as she shovels it away. She will clear some now, and then come back out later to start all over again. My father is at work and won't return until the next morning. It's supposed to snow until nighttime.

I breathe out with my mouth open, making a circle of fog on the glass. I trace my initials in the center, then wipe the glass clear and look at my mother. She is closer and I can hear her grunting as she lifts the heavy snow. Her back will be sore tonight, and she'll soak in a hot bath after she has settled us down for the night.

She stops. Leaning one arm on the shovel, rubbing her lower back with her other hand, she looks over at me.

"You should get up off the floor and away from that door. It's freezing. You're going to make yourself sicker."

"Shut up," I whisper. I want to yell it out to her, but I don't dare.

She goes back to work.

The snow flies through the air and sounds like baby kisses as it hits the glass of the door. I look at the tiny spots, each flake a miniature lace doily flattened against the glass; they stick and then fade away.

I open the door again and lean out.

"I want to come out in the snow! You have to let me!"

She stands in front of me, pulling the door open wider as she rests the shovel against the wall.

"Honey, you're sick. You have a fever. Please, stop whining and get away from the door. I'm coming in now."

I scoot back along the floor and out of her way. She stamps her feet on the doormat to knock off the snow, and then pulls her boots off as she steps inside.

"I hate you," I say.

She stops and stands still, staring straight ahead and saying nothing.

Again. "I hate you."

My mother turns and looks down at me, her eyes are tired, their lids heavy and slow. Her nose is red from the cold, her lips pale and chapped. She pulls the cap from her head. Her hair is wet with perspiration at the temples.

"You hate your mother? Because I won't let you go outside when you're sick? You hate me?" she says quietly. Then she walks past me, through the kitchen and into the foyer to hang up her wet jacket and lay her hat and gloves on the radiator.

I start to cry.

I want to call her back, tell her I'm sorry, that I didn't mean what I said. But I don't.

Instead, I stand and move back to the door, to watch the snow erase my mother's shoveled path. When it has disappeared completely, I am satisfied.

Vicki's mother (center, with hand on chin) and Vicki (foreground, with guitar)

Mirror

It is dark, but the street lamp shines a circle of light on the sidewalk in front of the house. A white colonial with a green roof and trim, it is set on the corner one block from a busy intersection, but the town is quiet now. It must be eight o'clock and it is a cold night. In a window of the house, just to the right of the front door, a table lamp glows brightly. Upstairs, all the windows are dark but for my parents' bedroom. The drawn shade is backlit and shadows move across it.

I am ten years old and my sister Debi is eight. We are getting ready to play beauty shop; the silhouettes floating on the scrim of the window shade are ours. Our father is at work for the night. Our baby sister, Terri, is asleep in the bedroom across the hall, and Eddie is sitting on the floor, his tiny green army men set up between the folds of the blanket that he has slid off the bed. He grumbles orders to the soldiers as he plays war, oblivious to us. With the dinner dishes done and our baths finished, my mother pulls the chair out from under my father's desk, moves it to the center of the room, and sits watching the television set atop the tall dresser in the corner.

"Make me beautiful, girls," she says.

"I get to do her hair," says Debi, as she grabs the pink-handled brush off the low dresser where my mother's hairspray and perfume, jewelry box, and framed family photos sit below the wide mirror on the wall.

"And I'll do her makeup," I say. I love to touch her skin. I find her makeup case on the dresser; it is beige, plastic, smudged with dirt, so full of lipsticks and eye shadows and compacts that the zipper has broken, and a fat rubber band is wrapped around it to keep everything from spilling out. I carry it to where my mother is sitting and place it in her hands on her lap.

The bedroom door is slightly ajar so she can hear if Terri wakes. Down the hall is my grandparents' bedroom, my father's

85

parents, and next to that room is where my great-grandmother sleeps, so we are quiet; we don't want to disturb them.

Our house is full of people; all day long there is work to be done. My father has two jobs and my mother cooks and cleans and my baby sister gets into things while Eddie, Debi, and I are at school. Grandma and Grandpa are always there, watching us with stern expressions, quick to scold if we make too much noise or run through the living room. My great-grandmother came here from Austria years ago; she never learned English and spends her days wandering the house, mumbling in German, often crying, wearing an old housedress and a dark kerchief on her head. Her blue eyes are huge, and so sad. By dinnertime my mother is tired and cranky and my father has to leave again to go back to work. But I know that soon we will go upstairs; she will sigh and relax, and we will have her to ourselves.

It is warm in this room. The TV glows and hums. Debi begins to brush our mother's long auburn hair. I can see Debi's face, so full of concentration, as she brushes smoothly, rhythmically. She is little, it is hard work for her, and I can hear her breathing. She looks at me smiling and crinkling her blue eyes.

"Look how nice I made her hair, it shines," she says.

"That's nice," I answer, and then I search inside the makeup case for the round puff of sponge I use to spread the creamy foundation over my mother's fair, freckled face. I hold the compact in one hand and the sponge in the other. I smell the makeup; it smells like my mother, it's the smell of her cheek as she bends down to kiss me goodnight. Now I touch the sponge to her skin, first to her forehead, then around her eyes, down her nose, her cheeks and chin. Her freckles disappear.

"I want to tease you," Debi says, as she puts the brush back on the dresser.

"Honey, here, use this," my mother says, pulling the rat-tailed comb out of her makeup case.

I put mascara on her eyelashes as Debi pulls up strands of her hair and combs them into knots. I am coating her lashes until they are thick and heavy, and I think to myself how much they look like spider legs now.

"My eyelids are getting stuck together," she says, blinking, fluttering her lashes as she laughs.

Green eye shadow to match her green eyes. Bright pink lips and cheeks. Her hair is big now; it is puffed out around her head like cotton candy.

"I'm done," Debi says.

"Can I look?" my mother asks.

I stand back, inspecting her. Debi moves next to me.

"What do you think?" I ask my sister.

"Very good."

"Okay," I tell my mother.

Then she stands up, arches her back and groans. Slowly she turns and walks to her dresser. She smiles into the mirror.

"I look gorgeous," she says, and Debi and I can't believe how beautiful she is.

Later, in my bed, waiting to fall asleep, I hear her in the bathroom, the water running as she washes her face.

This Night

Many afternoons my mother opened a can of beer and poured it into the green glass mug. Sometimes I'd watch as she enjoyed that first sip. Often she drank straight on until bedtime. She wasn't getting drunk; she was just unwinding. That was her word, unwinding.

I am keeping my mother company as she cleans up the dinner dishes. I must be about fifteen. It feels like late autumn, cold outside but toasty in the kitchen. On this night she isn't just drinking her beer. I see the tiny glass sitting on the kitchen counter, next to the sink. There is a drop of golden liquid in the glass. The Scotch bottle sits nearby.

"They can all go to hell. I tell you, straight to hell. I just can't take it anymore." My mother is sobbing as she scrubs the roasting pan. I am standing in the bright fluorescent light, leaning against the refrigerator, watching her shoulders shake as soap suds splash over the side of the sink and onto the floor.

Our house is not a happy one. Most evenings we all sit at the dining room table for the meal my mother has cooked. Sometimes we talk about school or friends with our parents. There are times when we laugh and play guessing games. But my grandparents and my great-grandmother just sit there; they always eat in silence.

Maybe that night there had been complaints. My father might have been unhappy because dinner wasn't ready on time; he is hungry and can't be late for work. When not at the firehouse, he is a cashier and deliveryman for a liquor store. Perhaps earlier in the day my grandfather had scolded my mother because my brother had left his toys on the living room floor, or my grandmother had complained to her that she couldn't nap because I was playing my stereo too loud. Or my great-grandmother had escaped again, wandering the neighborhood in her slip, making us cry to our mother with embarrassment, and rousing my grandfather's anger so that he would drag his mother back home and hit her.

"You're the only one who cares, the only one who listens," my mother says to me, looking over her shoulder with wet, bloodshot eyes.

She turns back to the sink, as if suddenly embarrassed.

"You should be upstairs, getting ready for bed. Why are you still down here anyway?"

"It's only nine o'clock," I tell her. I don't say how I wish I were upstairs, under my blanket, drifting off to sleep. I don't tell her that seeing her cry, watching her drink like this, makes me shiver even as I stand here in this warm kitchen.

"Are the rest of them ready for bed?"

"Yes. Terri's in bed already. Eddie and Debi are in your room, watching TV."

I walk to the door that separates the kitchen from the dining room and shut it. I know the looks they will throw at her back tomorrow morning, as they whisper to each other about this daughter-in-law who has made their son's life so difficult.

"I hate for you to see me like this. But really, I'm fed up. It's too much. None of you," her voice grows louder, harsher, "none of you gives a shit. I'm worn out, I tell you, I can't go on like this."

"Mom, I'm sorry. I know we don't help enough…"

"Ha! That's a laugh. Help? Help? What a joke. You're all a bunch of lazy bums."

"Mom, let me wash. I'll clean up the rest." I walk over and stand next to her at the sink. I'm nearly as tall as she is. I look at her cheek, wet, red, and blotchy.

She closes her eyes and cries more. She covers her face with her soapy hands.

"I'm sorry. You shouldn't see me like this. I'm just so lonely," she tells me. "It's not you. Not you, not my kids."

She puts her hands down and looks at me. Her eyes flit around, they're jumpy in their sockets, glassy, and I can see the red blood vessels whirling out from the green and gold centers, webs already spun. Then she turns and moves closer to the bottle. With shaking

89

hands she unscrews the top and pours a sloppy shot into the small glass.

She takes a sip this time, walking to the table in the alcove around the corner. I follow, watching her drag her feet as if she is pulling weights along behind her. She sways slightly before she collapses into a chair.

"Here, sit with me," she says, pulling out the chair next to her.

The vinyl padding of the seat sighs as I slide onto it. The light is off in here and we leave it that way. The darkness is comforting. We lean our elbows on the gray Formica tabletop, resting our chins in the palms of our hands. She is quiet, staring down at the shot glass, half empty now. I wonder if she's had enough.

I touch the top of her head, lightly, letting a few strands of her long, auburn hair wrap around my fingers. Only at home, in the evening, does she let her hair hang loose. Usually it is tamed into a prim and proper bun. I lift my hand and move it downward, slowly, combing with my fingers. This is what she used to do for me when I lay in bed with fever, or when a bad dream woke me in the middle of the night.

"Ahhh… that feels nice," she says, closing her eyes.

She bends forward, my fingers get tangled in her hair, and I hear her face slap against the tabletop. She begins to cry hard.

"Mom, what's wrong? Do you want to go up to bed now?"

She sits up quickly and pushes her chair out to stand, knocking it backward and onto the floor.

I follow her as she stomps back into the kitchen. She starts throwing pots and pans into a cupboard.

"My mother didn't want me," she says. "She didn't want to have me. I came too soon, they had no money and she didn't want me."

She's making too much noise. I worry that my grandparents will hear and come to investigate. She sits on the floor in front of the pot closet and begins rearranging the contents.

"No goddamn room. We have too much shit in here."

"Mom, not now. It's late. Clean it out in the morning."

"I have to get rid of something," she says.

"Not now," I tell her, reaching out my hand for her as she stands back up again.

"Let's go to bed," I say.

She is looking at me. "She didn't want me."

"Mom, I want to go to bed." I feel young. I am young. And tired. I don't want to take care of her anymore.

"She jumped in the lake. It was winter. She wanted to die so she wouldn't have to have me."

"Who are you talking about? Who jumped in a lake?"

"Mommy. Mommy. Some fishermen pulled her out."

I hear her say "Mommy" and I begin to cry.

"Why didn't she want me?"

She turns and walks to the sink. I am looking at her back again. She holds onto the sink with both hands, her arms straight and stiff. Her shoulders are shaking.

"And, do you know how I found out?" she says. I can barely hear her. "I was a little girl. And my grandmother showed me this newspaper article about an attempted suicide. She had cut it out and saved it. There was my mother's name, in that article. We were in her bedroom and she took it out of her desk drawer and showed it to me. Why? Why would she do that?"

"I don't know."

"My grandmother told me that my mother wanted to die because of me."

"Not because of you. She loved you, Mom. You know that." My mother talks about her mother often; from those stories she has told me, I know how close they were, how loving was their relationship.

She is quiet. Her elbows relax, she breathes in deeply.

"Yes. I know. But..."

She stops. I wait for her to keep speaking, but no more words come. She turns and walks to me. When she wraps her arms around me, I nestle my head in the crook of her neck. Then we stand apart, wiping our faces dry on our sleeves, looking at each other sideways, with shy smiles. I turn out the lights while Mom checks the lock on the front door. I walk up the stairs behind her, making sure she doesn't trip and fall.

Pat Malits, pregnant with Vicki, with her mother, Anna Boyle

Mother and Daughter

"This is your grandmother," my mother says.

I am about four years old. It is early in the morning. My father has left for work and my brother and sister are still asleep. I am curled next to my mother as she lies in her bed, my head on her chest. I look to where her finger points, a black-and-white snapshot, a small square of lights and darks. She holds the photo album on her belly. The pages are black and the pictures are held in place by white paper triangles glued at their corners.

We will do this often, look at the photographs, as my mother tells me stories about her mother.

There is the one from a New Year's Eve party. My grandmother is wearing pearls and my grandfather's arm is tight around her waist. They are looking at each other, smiling. Her hair falls down her back in waves. And I see a faint halo of wayward strands encircling her head.

"Her hair was red, long, and curly," my mother says. "Most of the time she kept it braided and twisted up in back. But when she wanted to look pretty, she would brush and brush, and I would help her. She'd wear it loose."

Then she tells me how the curls always came back, no matter how long and hard they brushed her hair, trying to make it smooth.

She turns the page. More pictures, more stories. Over and over, through the years, my mother and I sitting with the photographs, remembering her.

I was a year and half when my grandmother died. My mother was twenty-two and her mother was only forty-five. Even though I was just a baby when she died–suddenly, because a blood clot lodged in her brain–I like to think I can remember her. My mother talked about her constantly, never allowing the passing years to steal away the closeness they had shared.

A rainy summer afternoon when I am eight years old, and I am bored. My best friend, Janie, is away on vacation. Donna, my next best friend, is at camp. I leave my Barbie in my room and go downstairs. I see my mother in the living room, lying on the sofa, an ashtray on the floor beside her. Her knees are bent and she has the photo album propped up against her legs. She turns a page with one hand and rubs her cigarette out in the ashtray with the other.

"Come here," she tells me. "Look at this."

I walk over and sit on the floor next to her. She removes the photograph from its corners and hands it to me.

The color has faded and the edges are torn. It is a picture of my newborn self in my grandmother's arms.

"Mommy was so young," my mother says. "She was only forty-three when you were born."

I see the gray beginning at my grandmother's temples, but her hair is still red. It is held away from her face with a blue-and-white checked headband. I know this photograph well. In the picture I am a tiny face surrounded by white ruffles, and I stare up at her. Her mouth is open, as if she were in the middle of speaking.

"Look at you," my mother is saying as she turns toward me and peers at my face. "Your eyes... just like Mommy's."

She sits up, putting the photo album on the cushion next to her, and reaches for the pack of cigarettes on the side table.

"She would have loved to see you now, see how pretty you are," she says as she lights a match, holds it to the tip of the cigarette, and inhales.

"Do you miss her?" I ask.

"Every day."

It is late, the house is quiet. I can't sleep because of my period cramps and now my mother and I are sitting on the floor in her bedroom. I press a hot-water bottle to my belly. We sit on a folded blanket, resting our backs on pillows propped up against the side of the bed. We are close together, the photo album shared across our laps. The small lamp on the nightstand shines soft light down on us. My father is asleep, snoring.

"I used to walk all the way from our apartment on Sherwood Terrace, in Yonkers, to Bronxville, to visit Mommy at work," my mother tells me. I know this already; she has told me many times before.

"And I used to call her Mommy just like you did, right? I wouldn't say Grandma," I say.

"You thought she was your other mother."

In the photograph I am sitting in a baby buggy, wearing a white bonnet with a lacy frill surrounding my chubby face. My eyes are two dark slits, my nose and cheeks scrunching up as I chew down on a frozen, pink hot dog. Behind the carriage my grandmother is standing in the doorway of the butcher shop, wiping her hands on the red-stained white apron she wears, smiling proudly.

I turn to my mother on this night and see her tears; I am surprised by how they frighten me. Quickly I get up from the floor, whispering to her that I feel better now, that I am going back to bed. She does not move or speak, and I leave her there with her tears. In my bed, in the dark, I try to push away that image, my mother crying.

I grow busy and older, concerned more about friends and worries about my future than the family I still live with, the mother I love but seem now to disregard. High school graduation has passed and I am working as a bank teller in town. My mother is occupied with my three younger siblings, and she is struggling to give me over to adulthood. There are moments when I notice the look of loneliness on her face, hear the sighs of fatigue or annoyance she lets escape as I brush by her, on my way out the door.

"You don't know what it is like to miss your mother," she tells me one night, when I come home late, a little drunk, exhausted but happy after a night of bar hopping with friends. She is sitting in the TV room, crocheting another afghan; the yarn is gold and brown. She is still dressed, jeans and a pink sweatshirt, her legs crossed and her feet tucked under her, the white socks hidden from view. The room is dark save for the glow of the lamp on the end table and the light from the television. She looks cozy in the corner of the sofa; she looks like a young girl.

"I know," I say.

"It never goes away, missing her," she says, looking at me.

She's tired. I know she has waited up for me. She cannot sleep until I am safe at home. It annoys me, that she can make me feel this way, guilty, and sorry for her. I think about leaving her there, going up to bed. But I sit down next to her and let her talk to me.

Lies

When, all those years later, my mother told me that yes, she had been the ghost in the basement–the one that had haunted me for years, because I knew she must have been lying to me–well, I guess it was a relief. I was five years old, playing with my brother, sister, and cousins, running in and out of the cellar from the backyard. This was when we lived in the three-family house next to the train tracks in Bronxville. The landlord hated when we played down in the cellar, and it was dark and crowded with tools and piles of junk. Mom yelled for us to stop, but we ignored her. Then, on our next trip down the cellar steps we bumped into a ghost–tall and white and spreading out its arms, howling. We all ran out screaming, and I went inside to the kitchen where my mother and aunt sat, folding laundry. Sheets and towels. Mom was breathing heavily.

"Was that you?" I asked her, and she denied it with a smile. She had always told me lying was a sin, so I wanted to believe her.

I was a teenager when she finally admitted the truth about being the ghost, and I thought it had been a charming lie.

By then I had perfected the use of deceit. I could look straight into her eyes, unblinking, giving nothing away. I almost believed my own lies. Maybe that's the trick–convince yourself: it's not a lie, it's just not the whole truth.

"Yes, I was at the show, I can't help it if Mrs. Rooney says she didn't see me."

I was a seventh grader then, at Immaculate Conception School, and had just been dropped off by my friend's mother after the church's Easter pageant. Mom was outside with my sister Terri; they were planting flowers along the front walkway. Mrs. Rooney waved Mom over to the car. They talked for a few minutes and then she walked back to where I was standing.

"She says you disappeared as soon as the lights went out. She saw you get out of your seat. You didn't come back."

"I sat in a different spot."

"Why?"

"I had to go to the bathroom. I didn't want to walk back to the front."

Most of her wanted to believe me.

Was I at the show? Yes, for a few minutes. But then I turned and saw Joey McDonald standing in the back of the auditorium; he waved to me, gestured for me to come to him. I did, and we snuck up the back staircase and into the church proper, then climbed the spiral steps to the choir loft. Sitting on the kneeler, our backs against the pew in front of us, we kissed. My first official make-out. As he pushed his tongue between my lips, I prayed the wad of gum stuck to the roof of my mouth wouldn't come loose.

Such a little thing, hiding this from my mother. And it was necessary, I believed. If I had told the truth the consequences would have been earth-shattering: first, her anger, her disappointment, and my shame; then the punishment, surely a grounding, possibly for two weeks or more. Anyway, it was my life, my decision to miss the show and sneak off with Joey. She wouldn't understand.

Tony Porto's birthday party. "Yes, Mom, his parents will be there. And I think his aunt and uncle." But they weren't. Just thirty or so fourteen- and fifteen-year-olds, and Tony's older sister; she bought the wine. I remember drinking from the bottle each time one was passed to me. Boone's Farm Apple Wine. The first few sips were difficult; the wine was warm, and tasted sour, but I glugged it down. Made out with Brad, and then Dominick. Joanie Grogan was lying in the middle of the living room floor, eyes closed, barefoot in her blue flowered peasant dress.

Mom picked us up at eleven, my best friend Alice and me, the latest I had been allowed to stay out so far. We chomped frantically on our minty chewing gum.

"I'm not an idiot, you know," Mom said. "You think I don't know you're trying to cover up the booze on your breath?"

We said nothing. Neither did she for the rest of the ride. Alice was sleeping over, and after we both stumbled and giggled our way up to my bedroom, we shut the door and I waited for Mom, but she didn't come. The next morning, after Alice had left, I went to her in the kitchen, to apologize.

"I'm sorry, I only had a few sips, I..."

Without looking at me she said, "No. Stop. I don't want to hear it. Just go away."

I wasn't sure what it was that she didn't want to hear—more lies, or the truth.

She lied to me too, though. A silly ghost in the basement. But mostly it was those white lies of omission. Maybe it was by osmosis that I learned not everything had to be revealed. Sometimes you just told a person what you thought they needed to hear.

"Yes, you look very nice," she told me when I asked if I looked okay, being new to putting on makeup. I was probably just fifteen, and used only mascara and blush. She was setting the dining room table for lunch. My father's aunt, Helen, a beautician, was coming to visit that afternoon. I helped fold the napkins and put them by each place setting.

The doorbell rang and in walked Aunt Helen, blonde beehive and fox fur stole.

Hugs and kisses for Mom. Then she turned to me and asked, "What happened to your face? Your cheeks are so red!"

Embarrassed, but grateful, I went upstairs to fix my makeup before I went out later with my friends. I remember seething, though, at my mother's lie, her attempt to avoid criticizing or hurting me. She did that, tried to protect me, giving half answers to my questions. Her explanations, always offered with love, were not to be trusted.

There was my father's uncle. I was small, maybe six or seven, when I walked into the kitchen to see my mother pressed up against the closet door by his two tanned hands, with their bumpy knuckles, on her breasts. She was turning her head to the side, avoiding his lips, puckered and shiny-wet. She saw me and lifted her knee, kicking him between the legs, forcing him to back away.

"We're just playing, joking around," she said, taking my hand, leading me back into the living room where the company sat, drinking and talking. Five or so years later, when that uncle came up behind me in the kitchen, putting his arms around my waist and his hands on my new breasts, I remembered what she had said. I couldn't believe she thought this was just a joke. I froze. I waited. He kissed my neck and then let me go just as my father walked into the room. I never told my mother about it. I'd learned: not everything had to be revealed.

There were many things I never told her. With time it seemed I had more to hide than my mother did. I was sliding away from her, keeping her at a distance.

Late one weekend night–I was twenty by then–I stopped home from a date to pick up my diaphragm. I tried not to wake her as I searched behind the shoeboxes on my closet floor. After I found the bag I kept it in, I rushed back out to my boyfriend's car. When I came home a couple of hours later, my mother was in my room, sitting on my bed in the dark. I was stoned. I turned on the overhead light. Whatever she was about to confront me with, I was in no shape to handle.

"What is this for?" she asked, holding out the plastic applicator that I used with my diaphragm.

"What are you doing with that?"

"I found it in your closet. I heard you rummaging around in there," she said.

I couldn't believe she had gone into my closet, checking to see what I had been up to. I couldn't believe she was asking me what it was; didn't she know? Did she really think I wasn't having sex? I became transfixed by her face, her expression. She looked frightened; she looked childlike. I felt I knew what she was thinking. She was hoping I would tell her something she could believe.

"It's for my yeast infection. It was for putting the medicine in."

"Oh. So what did you come home for earlier?"

"I changed my shoes. My feet were hurting."

She got up and left my room then. She seemed satisfied.

When I was older, married, a mother myself, we began to reveal some of our mutual prevarications. She was shocked to learn I had had sex at fourteen. I was disappointed to find out she had read some of my diaries. She expressed a surprising curiosity about how it felt to smoke weed.

When we embarked upon this new openness, did that mean we were completely honest with each other? Of course not.

On the day my mother found out she had pancreatic cancer–inoperable, incurable–I sat on her hospital bed and looked her straight in the eye.

"You are going to be okay. I will find a way to make you better," I told her.

She looked away.

Gentle Woman

I walk through the front door of the house where I grew up, and into the familiar kitchen. Aunt Sis is sitting on an old wooden stool in the middle of the big bright room. Her hands are folded in her lap, her head is tilted back, eyes closed, her face lit by the fluorescent ceiling light. She is my mother's aunt, eighty years old, and still her skin is silken.

"Hold still," my mother says.

She is bending forward, leaning in close to Sis's face, one hand on her forehead and the other guiding the razor across her aunt's chin. There is a mint-green bath towel wrapped around Aunt Sis's shoulders, to catch the drips from her wet and slicked-back hair. My mother must have just given her a shampoo in the sink. Her hair is glossy black with white streaks like stripes, and cut short like a man's. The shaving cream on her chin looks like a small beard.

It's almost six and I've decided to stop by on my way home from work. The apartment I live in is just ten minutes from here, and my boyfriend, Bill, whom I live with, won't be getting home until later. I'm thinking that maybe my mother has made a dinner I can share.

She looks up and smiles.

"Hey! Nice surprise," she says.

"I thought you'd be eating dinner," I say.

"I have a meatloaf in the oven. Stay. Eat. It'll be ready in about a half-hour."

"Dad home?"

"Lying down, upstairs."

I walk to the table, pull a chair close to where my mother is, and sit.

"Hi, Sis," I say.

"Don't talk," my mother tells Sis. "I don't want to cut you."

"Sorry," I say.

My mother's hand shakes. Her hands always shake, and still she is good with her hands, capable, sure of herself. She is concentrating now; she is being careful, gentle.

"How's work?" she asks.

I tell her about the new exhibits opening at the museum and about the artists' lecture series I'm working on for spring. When she finishes shaving Sis's chin, she takes the towel to wipe first her own hands and then Sis's face.

"Okay, now let's get you upstairs and into the shower before I have to get dinner on the table," she tells Sis.

She looks up at me. "So, are you staying? Come upstairs, we can talk more."

My mother misses her children. She is only forty-nine and we are all out of the house. Eddie moved out first, at nineteen, into an apartment over a garage in a town nearby, where my mother goes to take care of his three cats when he's away. Debi got married a year ago, to the boyfriend she had been living with for five years. And Terri is an hour away, living with another girl, working as a paramedic. It is a time when my mother should be free to come and go as she pleases, yet it has turned out that not only is she caring for her senile aunt who has moved in, but her mother-in-law, my widowed grandmother, is still living in the house. She has a bad heart and a frail body, and spends much of her time lying down, but her mind is quick and her will formidable.

Sis stands and walks toward the staircase in the foyer. She is tall, with the straight and strong back of a much younger woman. My mother likes to say that if you took Sis's healthy body and my grandmother's sharp mind, you'd end up with one whole person.

"How are you doing, Sis?" I ask, following her, and she smiles and keeps walking, repeating in a singsong voice, "Fine and dandy, fine and dandy."

The three of us climb the steps and go into Sis's bedroom. As my mother helps Sis out of her clothes and into her robe, I sit on the bed and look away. There are rosary beads of clear-cut crystal with a silver chain and cross on the nightstand, and a small black-

and-white photograph in an old brass frame—a middle-aged Sis with my mother and her sister as children.

She walks Sis down the hall to the bathroom. "Now remember to wash good," she says. "Get under your arms and between your legs. I'm going to come in and check and I want to see you soapy. Don't just stand in there daydreaming."

While Sis showers, my mother and I sit on the bed to talk. I can smell the meatloaf baking in the oven and I feel hungry. She is asking me if Bill and I have had any more conversations about getting married.

"You know, I told him to please make me a mother-in-law before making me a grandmother."

"Don't worry," I tell her, knowing, but not saying, that becoming a mother is the farthest thing from my mind.

"I'll be right back," she says, as she pats my knee and gets up to check on Aunt Sis.

My stomach growls. I am looking forward to the meatloaf.

Vicki's mother with her grandson, Billy

Selfish

"This is supposed to be one of the happiest times of your life. What the hell is wrong with you?" With that, my mother walked out of my apartment, leaving me at the kitchen window.

The tone of her voice was familiar—impatient, disgusted. She never could tolerate anybody wallowing in self-pity. I'd let myself tell her how I was feeling, somehow convincing myself that this time she would be able to help me. But instead she left.

I stood at the window, holding my son, my newborn, firstborn. He had come into the world five days earlier, with spring's arrival, at the crack of dawn. I was thirty-four years old. After an hour of pushing, when the doctor placed my gooey, blood-bathed baby on my belly, and I heard his shaky mewing cries, my heart cracked and I immediately wanted him back inside of me. Suddenly he was real, and the responsibility, the love even, overwhelmed me, became threatening. While I was pregnant, he'd been a dream, make-believe, and he had been so easy.

Now I was crying, and I couldn't stop. My baby was asleep, his head on my shoulder, his small body folded against me as if attached, still part of me. Out the window I watched the breeze rock the tree branches, tickling the fresh leaf buds.

Billy was fair-skinned, with an orange fuzz covering his bruised head. He was scrunchy-faced and so cute, and you could tell he was his father's son. Something about the eyes. He didn't look anything like me. I sniffled as snot ran over my lips.

Mom adored her new grandson. Since I'd gotten home from the hospital she came by every day. She'd hold Billy, giving me time to shower and dress. She never noticed that I'd been crying all morning. I tried to control myself before she arrived, but in the shower I'd let loose again. It seemed there was no end to the amount of tears I could shed. I felt like an idiot. I felt ashamed. I didn't understand why I was so unhappy.

In April of 1956, my mother was a bride. In May, when she got her period, she cried. But the next month it did not come, and I was born the following March. She was happy. Thirteen months later my brother, Eddie, was born. And in September of 1959, Debi arrived. Twenty-four years old, the mother of three children under the age of three, she was exactly where she wanted to be.

As I stroked Billy's tiny back I thought about the many times she had said that having children was the best thing about her life.

I was hungry. I was still wearing my nightgown at three in the afternoon. But I was afraid to put the baby down in his bassinet. He might wake up. Then I'd have to nurse him again. My nipples were sore. I was so sleepy. And I was bored. And lonely.

"Daddy will be home in a couple of hours," I whispered. The baby ignored me.

That evening, my husband, Bill, videotaped me while I was on the telephone with my mother. Since our baby had arrived, he was rarely without the camera in his hands. That same night, we watched the video. Following scenes of Billy sleeping, being changed, nursing, lying on the bed blinking up at the eye of the camera, there is me. I am sitting in the rocking chair, Billy cooing in my arms, the telephone cradled against my shoulder. You can only hear my side of the telephone conversation, but there is also Bill's gentle narration. I am tearful and sobbing throughout.

"I know I'm supposed to be joyful. I have a healthy, beautiful baby. He's really so good. But all I can do is worry. I worry all the time," I am saying. I don't realize he is filming me.

Bill's voice: "Isn't she adorable? She doesn't realize how adorable she is when she's crying. Poor baby. She's so tired."

"I can't help it." My voice is strained, defensive. "I don't know! I don't know why I feel like this!"

Bill: "I wish she could just relax. I wish she would realize it's going to be okay."

"I know! I know! But I guess you were a better mother than me!"

As I watched, I realized how much I had wanted to hear my husband's words from my mother. Instead, her words during that phone call were the same as those she'd spouted earlier in the day.

"How selfish can you possibly be?" she'd said. "Why are you feeling sorry for yourself, when you have a baby to care for?"

The smile she wore for the baby had faded, and her eyes narrowed, as if she were trying harder to see me. As she stared at me I looked down, at her bright, white sneakers.

I tried to explain, but it was difficult. Like many times in the past, my emotions did not belong to words; my mind had abandoned rational thought, had become a soup of sensation instead. Nothing seemed clear, and everything I was thinking became a feeling, wet and sticky, heavy and thick.

"I don't feel sorry for myself. Maybe I feel sorry for him," I said. "I can't be a mother. I don't know how. I...I think I made a mistake."

"Well, it's a little late now," she said.

Billy stirred in my arms. "Shush," I whispered in his ear.

"He's five days old, for God's sake! How much work can he possibly be?" She was reaching for her pocketbook, her denim jacket, getting ready to leave. "And then you say in the next breath that this is boring? Taking care of a baby is boring!"

"Mom, don't go yet. I'm sorry. It's just that I never thought it would be this hard."

"Hard? This is hard? You have no idea how hard life can be!"

"Please...What should I do?" I asked.

"Get a grip!" she yelled.

And then, more quietly, speaking to herself, "I can't take this."

My mother had handled a lot. When we were little, my brother, sisters, and I, there was always some catastrophe brewing. She must have visited the emergency room scores of times with one or another of us, Eddie especially. She'd joke, "They should name a wing of the hospital after me, I'm there so much."

Illnesses, injuries—she was wonderful at taking charge, at doling out necessary remedies and relief. Yes, a cut and blood, vomit, or a clogged nose, these were worthy of sympathy and comfort. Even bruised feelings after an argument with a friend, or the heartbreak of losing a favorite toy, were worthy. But anything that lasted longer than the momentary hurt and a few tears, well, that was going too far.

And I was a child prone to dark moods. I'm not sure when it began, but I often found myself overwhelmed by fear, sadness, a feeling of loneliness that found no salve in company. I would look at my mother and see her as if I were looking at her through the wrong end of a telescope. I would slide down into the gloom and she would move away, out of reach. I was occupying a realm she couldn't, or wouldn't, approach. As close as we were, as much as I clung to her, when those moods came over me a wall of ice shot up between us.

I remember being fourteen and it was autumn. I was glad the weather had cooled. I liked a chill in the air; I liked to shiver a bit and then bundle up in my new sweaters bought for a new school year and make myself a cup of sweet tea and go to my room to read. But the shorter days, the darker afternoons, they made me feel sad, and now the upstairs hallway was conspiring against me. Mom had painted it brown. Every morning when my day began and every evening when my day came to an end I walked the brown corridor. It seemed longer, cavernous, and it was so dark.

It was early in the evening on a Friday. I was dressed to go out, to meet my boyfriend on the corner and walk to the pizza parlor and hang out. I stood outside my bedroom door, in the upstairs hallway, and my mother stood at the other end. She was in front of her bedroom door, a basket of dirty laundry under one arm, balanced on her hip. She was complaining. She looked tired—she always looked tired and seemed never to rest. Her long hair was pulled back into a ponytail, and her fair, freckled face, naked now that she had washed off her makeup, was pallid in the dark of the hallway. She wore her wine-colored housecoat and she was barefoot. I didn't want to look at her. It made everything so much worse when I looked at her.

"Where do you think you're going? Ready for a night on the town? Well, have fun, and don't worry about me, cleaning up your mess and doing your laundry."

"Leave it," I said. "Don't wash my clothes. I'll do it tomorrow."

"What about the towels?" she shouted. "Every time you take a goddamned shower you use two new clean towels. Every other day I'm washing towels."

"I'll do them tomorrow."

"Forget it, just go out."

She turned to go downstairs.

"No!" I screamed. "No, no, no!"

She stopped and turned back.

"No!" I screamed louder. "No!" Again and again I screamed.

She was looking at me carefully, searching my face.

"Stop it," she whispered, and a smile, new and sharp, changed her face, made it hard.

"Stop it," she repeated. But I didn't.

I was just screaming now. I leaned forward, throwing those sounds toward her.

"You're an idiot, that's all. A crazy idiot," she said. She turned away and walked down the stairs with the laundry.

I leaned back against the brown wall and slid down to the floor. I didn't go out that night. When I didn't show up on the corner, my boyfriend came and rang the doorbell. I heard Mom talking to him, the murmur of their voices. She probably told him I wasn't feeling well.

I sat there, in the hallway, for about an hour. I began to think about the last time I had played house. It must have been about three years earlier. I remembered going down to the basement where my sisters and I and our friends had set up little homes with old furniture and toys. Our dolls were down there. I was alone. I was good at playing alone. I could make-believe for hours. But that day nothing worked. The dolls weren't babies and the basement was damp and everything looked messy. As much as I wanted to, I couldn't pretend, and it seemed like the saddest thing in the world. I thought about that, as I sat in the hallway that day when I was fourteen, my back against the brown wall.

Years later, I went for help. I learned about clinical depression, obsessive-compulsive disorder, anxiety disorder. Back when I had held Billy in my arms and cried ceaselessly, I had no words for that dark place.

My postpartum depression lasted for quite a while. Mom would still come over to help out now and then, and I would drive to her house to visit. But I cried at home, alone, every day. Bill was ever patient, gentle with me. I believe I survived that painful time because of him. Eventually, I cried less. I tried to push the guilt into the background; it was tough and stubborn, rearing its ugly head every so often. But I was doing it, taking care of my son, and he was well, he was happy.

"Come to Grandma, cutie-pie."

I handed Billy over as I walked through her front door. It was late May, a hot spring day. Billy's chubby bare legs kicked with excitement as he slid from me to my mother.

"So big and handsome," she told my baby as she carried him over to the sofa and sat holding him out in front of her.

For the rest of the day, as we walked around the lake in the park, did grocery shopping together, went back to her house where she gave Billy a bottle, I carried a clump of thorns inside my chest, but did not let the tears flow. I noticed how Mom never once looked at or spoke directly to me. For now, the baby was our point of connection, and our excuse for ignoring the wall of ice.

The Painting

My boys are four and two the summer my mother throws out one of her paintings. It is a big one, a scene of a lake and trees, surrounded by a handmade frame she'd crafted from some old pieces of ceiling molding. She's on one of her crazed clean-out-all-the-crap kicks, and she has decided that this particular painting is crap. So there it sits, on top of a pile of rickety furniture and dust-caked knickknacks, out by the side of the road in the bright hot afternoon sun.

As I pull my red station wagon alongside the curb, Mom gives me her big smile, wiping her dirty hands across her jeaned thighs. From the back seat Billy and Steven start yelling, "Hi, Grandma!"

Mom helps me unbuckle the boys and haul them out of the car.

"What you doing, Grandma?" Billy asks.

"Cleaning. I have a lot of old stuff I need to throw away."

"Mom, that painting, it's been hanging over the living room sofa for years. Why'd you decide to get rid of it now?" I ask.

"I never liked it," she says.

I think about taking it, but honestly, I'd never liked it either. There didn't seem to be anything special about it. It was like one of those generic landscapes you see in the furniture department of Macy's.

The boys and I head around to the back of the house to spend the rest of the day playing in the pool. My parents had bought an above-ground pool, four feet deep, twenty-four feet round, a few years earlier. "For our grandchildren," my father said.

"I'll join you guys soon as I finish with this mess," Mom says.

My father rarely comes out to the yard, hardly ever goes in the water. He's content to pass his summer days in the air-conditioned TV room watching baseball and golf. Mom says he'd sit and watch a tiddlywinks match if that were the only sport on television.

Mom is like a big kid, though. She loves the water and spends so much time in the pool that she gets those crinkly-wrinkled fingertips and toes all the time. Usually when we arrive at her house on summer days I find her out back, half asleep on a blow-up float, one hand dangling off the side playing with the water. The sun shines on her multicolored bathing suit, emphasizing its fluorescence, and her fair skin looks tan from the crowding of all her freckles.

Once her grandsons arrive, though, that is the end of her relaxation. They climb the ladder in a hurry, pulling at each other, trying to be the first one to jump in and splash Grandma.

We aren't in the pool long that day before Mom joins us. "My back is killing me," she says as she slides off the side of the deck and into the water.

"You finished throwing out all your junk?" I say.

"I'll finish later. I thought I'd give you a break, play with the kids."

My boys are already good swimmers, but as soon as Mom is in the pool, they cling to her, taking turns riding on her back, and then climbing up on the deck and jumping into her arms. Her energy seems endless, and I take full advantage of her generosity. Now I am the one lounging on the float, paddling my hands to steer clear of the commotion my boys make.

As I lie here, eyes closed, my mind drifting, I am pulled back by the laughter of my boys. I let her delight them; I need her to attend to them. On my own, alone at home with them, the episodes of joy, of innocent mayhem, are meager. Often bored with motherhood, missing my days working at the museum, my time with coworkers discussing exhibits and lectures, I know I am cheating them. When we are at home, I have schedules, rules, activities planned for them, and I can see my obsession for purposeful enterprise crowd out their playfulness.

My mother observes me. When she comes to my house, she comments on the orderliness, the quiet. "When you kids were little, our house looked like a tornado hit it," she'd say, and I take those words as an insult, the slight I believe she means them to be.

Now I float, and am happy that my boys are having fun.

A week later, in the grocery store, I run into Brenda, a friend of a friend. She stops me to tell me she took the painting off the pile of trash outside my parents' house, and it's now hanging in her dining room.

"You're kidding? My mother painted that!"

"Really? I love it."

"Well, now you know who the artist is," I say.

Mom is proud and thrilled when I tell her about Brenda and the painting.

"Wow, so someone liked it. That's nice. That's funny," she says.

We are sitting by the pool again, the boys in the water with my sister and her kids.

"Hey, Deb, did you hear that? Someone has my painting hanging in their house."

"Yeah. Vicki told me. I wish you'd told me you were getting rid of it."

"How come you didn't want it?" Mom asks me.

I am annoyed by the question.

"I don't know. I have nowhere to put it."

"You just didn't like it," she says, turning her face away, blowing cigarette smoke up to the sky.

"Well, neither did you. You didn't ask me if I wanted it anyway."

"It doesn't matter," she says, adding, "I know it's not your style."

Mom thought I was a snob when it came to her painting and her crafting. Because I had gone to college, and majored in art history, she assumed I thought myself too sophisticated to

113

appreciate her dabbling.

My going to college was still a touchy subject between us.

Back in my senior year of high school, as our family sat around the dining room table eating dinner, I told my mother and father about the parents' meeting for college that was coming up. My father spoke first.

"You're not going to college. We can't afford college. Besides, you're a girl; you're just gonna get married and have kids anyway."

Mom added, "Just get a good job, like your cousin, with health insurance."

Following her advice, I went ahead and got a job as a bank teller. But two years later, I quit. I wanted to go to college. Mom thought I was nuts.

"You have a good job, with benefits. Why would you quit?"

I applied for financial aid and loans, moved on campus, and after graduation I was hired at the university art museum. When again I had a good job, Mom apologized for not having been more supportive.

Once in a while, though, she still let it be known how she felt: my college degree made me act superior to her. And sometimes, that was true.

Two years later, September. My mother has been dead for three months.

This morning, I have an hour to do my exercise walk before it's time to pick up my boys from school. It is cool out, cloudy; the night before we had rainstorms, thunder, lightning. But now blue is beginning to peek out between the clouds, and I walk briskly along my usual route through town.

Climbing the hill of Stewart Place, up ahead on the left, in front of Brenda's house, I see a pile of soggy cardboard boxes leaking old books and magazines, a rocking chair with a broken leg, and my mother's painting. It sits on the ground facing the street, my mother's name brushed in white paint jumping out at me from the lower right hand corner. The frame has warped with the rain, and the image ripples across the canvas, splashed with mud.

I'd heard Brenda was moving. Obviously, my mother's painting is not going with her. I know I have to take it home, rescue it.

I stop and pick it up. It is heavy, and I have a long walk. I'll have to come back with my car, so I move it away from the road, onto the front lawn, and hope I get back before it is taken away.

I drive back with Billy and Steven. The painting is still lying on the grass. I lift it into my car by the passenger side door and slide it between the front seats, through to the back, between my boys.

"Guys, do me a favor, hold on to Grandma's painting, okay?"

"Okay," they say, each putting a little boy hand on the warped wood frame.

"You know what we're gonna do?" I say. "We're gonna get Grandma's painting cleaned up and put it in a new frame, and we can hang it in the living room. We can look at it every day."

Billy cocks his head to one side, examining the picture. "I like it," he says. "It's pretty."

Sunset

The suitcase has been sitting in the foyer, just inside the front door, for five days now. That is where my father left it when he came home the evening my mother died. It's hers, the one that went with her to the hospital three weeks ago. I pick it up; it's small, an overnight bag really. Not heavy. I carry it upstairs to my parents' bedroom, set it on the floor, and open it.

I pick up her eyeglass case. I hear my mother. "Where are my glasses? Anyone see my glasses?" Every day. Ten times a day, and usually they were on top of her head.

Her slippers. White terrycloth with embroidered roses at the toes, white rubber soles. I see her feet. She hated her feet, thought they were ugly, the second toe reaching out past the big toe, the nails painted bright pink or peach in defiance of their awkwardness. She wore Keds, Keds sneakers, all the time, the plain white ones, like a little girl.

I pull out her nightgowns. Blue, cotton, simple. They smell like her. I bury my face in them and close my eyes. I feel so sorry for them.

Her toothbrush. Her makeup case. Underpants. Socks.

I hear my husband's voice; he's in the backyard with our children. My boys are laughing. We are at my parents' house, the house where I grew up. We've walked here this afternoon for a visit. Our home is just three blocks away. The boys love to visit their grandparents, but now it's just Grandpa. I look up at the pictures hanging on the walls, landscapes painted by my mother. Canvases like these fill the house, the houses of relatives and friends. It was her hobby, her obsession, her escape—painting these idyllic scenes. A warm breeze blows in through the open window.

I look at her things spread out on the floor, and then I put everything back into the suitcase.

It will be several months before my father, brother, sisters, and I clean out her closet, her dresser, the small drawer of her night table.

I've kept two of her driver's licenses. One, June 12, 1992. Only a touch of gray. Her eyes look bigger than they were because of how wide open she holds them. She looks shocked. Her mouth is a short, straight line. A real mug shot.

The other. Issued May 8, 1996. Two days before she is diagnosed with cancer. She's grayer. Her face is thinner. She is smiling, a stretched out, forced smile. Forcing it. I know she's in pain. She had gone to the doctor a few days before because of the pain in her legs and back. Bed rest, a heating pad, Advil, was the prescription. While lying on the heating pad, her hands resting on her stomach, she felt a lump. A protrusion. She went for x-rays on May 10.

She got her new driver's license but she didn't need it. After the x-rays and the diagnosis, the exploratory surgeries, the radiation and the chemotherapy, she never drove again. She was always sick, always in pain.

There are moments that scratch at my memory. Like being in a bookstore one evening when my mother was sick. The first thing I see is a table display of new paperbacks. The latest book by a mystery writer Mom enjoys catches my eye. She loves his stories, reads every one of his books. All I can think is, "She'll never read this one. She'll never read another book."

It's Tuesday evening, June 10, 1997. My sister Debi and I have just arrived at the hospital, a five-minute ride from both our houses. We sit on Mom's bed, one of us on each side of her. We bend down to her ear and take turns whispering our love. She has her eyes closed; her bed is in an upright position and she's wearing an oxygen mask.

Auntie Ann, Mom's sister, up from Florida for the fourth time in the past year, had called us to say we should come quickly. Pulmonary edema. A matter of hours.

"Joey? Joey? Is Joey here?" Mom rasps. The ocean is in her chest. It churns. She is drowning in her own fluids.

"Here I am." My father's cousin gets up from a chair in the corner of the room and comes to the bed. Debi and I back away. We wait for the words my mom needs to tell him.

"Joey, I never got to see your new car."

We laugh. And I wonder why she cares, why does that matter? The hours stretch out into four more days.

I still see the hospital room. The pale yellow walls. The big window looking out over the village. The lone birthday card on the nightstand. "Happy Birthday to a Dear Aunt," sent by my cousin Kathy in Florida. She and her two sisters will begin their drive north early on Friday.

"My son? Where's my son?" Eddie, my brother. Mom reaches up to pull him closer. I can't hear what she is saying. His face is so soft, so sweet, so open. He is blushing.

Four nights later, I will be at home, but Eddie will be with her, holding her hand. And then, he will call me. "It's over," he'll say.

But, Tuesday night. Tuesday night. Her lungs keep filling up. The doctor and nurses try to drain them, put tubes up her nose and push them down into her lungs, but she fights them; it's too painful. "Why don't they just give me something; I'm dying. Why don't they just give me something?" But, when she can't get air, when she can't breathe, she reaches out desperately, her eyes bulging, grasping for her asthma inhaler. Dad tries to help. I stare at him. He has never looked so focused, or frightened. He looks younger. His skin shines and lies so smoothly over his bones and muscles. Frozen. While Mom thrashes about on the bed, he finds her inhaler, grabs her right hand and presses her fingers around it. "Here, Pat, here, honey. It's okay. Breathe. Breathe." He is breathing with her, for her.

Finally, they start the morphine drip and she can rest. She falls asleep. "Turn it up every hour," the doctor tells the nurses before

118

he leaves.

Moments gather into days. Four days.

The gaps between her breaths grow longer. With each labored inhalation, we sigh, and not with relief, but with pity. "It's okay, Pat, you can rest. Go home, Pat. We love you. It's okay," my aunt tells her sister.

In time, on Saturday night, after the storm has passed and the ocean has stilled, I sit alone with my father in his living room. He breaks down, his smooth, still face cracks and moves in quakes. I do something I have never done, something I never thought I could do. I hold him in my arms and let his wet cheek rest on my shoulder. "You were all telling her it was okay," he says. "You were all telling her to let go, to go home. You prayed for her to die. I, I was praying for a miracle."

My father sits next to her bed, hoping. He holds her hand and tells her, "You're so beautiful, Pat. You are my beautiful girl."

I sit on the opposite side and reach for her other hand. I have to fold her fingers for her. They are long, slender.

I picture her hands holding the paintbrush, the palette, mixing colors, and I watch her work in front of the canvas, painting the sky, bright and blue. She'll pick up a pencil, grab a scrap of paper and sketch. My little girl face on paper, torn and yellowed now. My mother's hands on the steering wheel as I watch from the back seat. Then, we're at the pool. She swims smoothly, each hand cutting the water in its turn, leading the way.

My mother's hands. I know both their gentleness and their strength.

And then, at seven in the evening, on Saturday, June 14, the day after her sixty-third birthday, my mother dies. "Peacefully," Eddie tells me over the phone.

I drive to the hospital. Park the car and ride the elevator to the fifth floor. I walk to her room. It is strangely quiet. I make my way past everyone else and stand by her bed. I collapse over her, and the sound I hear myself making surprises me. One part of me watches and listens as the other becomes primitive in grief.

She is still warm. My hands hold her shoulders and I feel the strong bones beneath the soft flesh. My face is nestled in the crook of her neck. I can smell her; she smells like my mother, she smells like comfort. I could stay here, like this, forever. I hear my sobs; they come from deep down, from years and years ago, from the day I was born. I want to stay here, I could sleep here, I need to hold her, I have to breathe her in.

I hear the silence of the room, the hushed sadness, the controlled anguish, and I hear my groans.

A hand on my shoulder, my sister's touch, startles me back. I become quiet. I sit up. My hands still hold her shoulders. I look at her face. So relaxed. A shimmer of spittle lies in the corners of her lips. She has been dead for half an hour.

"I have suffered the atrocity of sunsets." Sylvia Plath wrote that. I think this, this line of poetry sings inside my head. "I have suffered the atrocity of sunsets."

Day is coming to an end. My mother is gone. My father has cried on my shoulder. Our family has gathered together at his house. His house. My brother, sisters, cousins, aunt. My husband comes with our children.

"Mommy!" Billy cries as he climbs out of the car. He runs to me. I stand on the front lawn. I am looking up at the sky.

"Mommy, Daddy took us to get pizza. He let me have soda. Why didn't you come with us?"

Billy is six years old, blond and blue-eyed. I look at his face. I smile when I see the freckles across his cheeks and nose. Those are from his grandmother.

"I was at the hospital, visiting Grandma," I tell him.

Steven runs up to us. Three years old. Dark hair and brown

eyes. My mother's smile.

"Mommy, give me a kiss," he demands.

I sit down on the grass, hug him, kiss his cheek.

"Me, too, Mommy," Billy says, and I pull him onto my lap next to Steven. I am trying not to cry.

"Look at the sky," I tell them.

The sun is setting. And the sky is pink, purple, red, yellow, blue, orange.

"It looks like a painting," Billy says.

"A painting," says Steven.

"I bet Grandma painted the sky," I say. "She's up there now, you know, in heaven."

"Heaven?" Steven whispers.

"Did Grandma die?" Billy asks.

"Yes."

"Now?"

"A little while ago."

"Oh," he says quietly, looking up at the sky. "And she's in heaven?"

"Yes."

"And she painted the sky?" he asks, looking at me now, and I am looking at him.

"Maybe," I answer. "Yes. Why not, right?"

That's all I can tell him.

We sit quietly together. We watch the sky change.

Behind us, in the house, people are talking and crying, eating and drinking. They laugh quietly and then look confused, guilty. They try to comfort one another. Lamps are being turned on.

My boys squirm in my lap; I know they are getting tired.

"Let's go inside," I say.

As we walk into the house I feel the cool of the air-conditioning, I smell the sauce that simmers on the stove, and I notice the suitcase sitting there by the front door.

*L*ori

Lori's mother, Estella Mae Webb, at her wedding

Confluence

Sometimes when driving alone I'd think of my mother, and within seconds I'd be crying. It was 2006, and she had been gone a year, but I was still missing her from a deep place I didn't even know I held. I'd remember our more bitter moments and I'd find myself wishing I could correct whatever I had done to anger her. I wanted to give our relationship one more chance. Where was that quiet I hoped for, now that she couldn't rant on about how I was neglecting her?

I was not writing about her. As a subject, my mother, the woman of the past twenty years, felt too dense and unkind. I had plenty of other work to bring into our writers group. I came with fiction, short stories, and a few chapters from a novel, all of which I'd written over the past few years.

I have a small office upstairs, near my sons' bedrooms. My desk, by the window, overlooks the woods; a pine bookcase faces the desk. There's an armchair in the corner, where one of my three dogs naps every day; it was supposed to be my reading chair.

Before I joined the group, I worried that I'd become so immersed in my work that I'd drive myself into isolation. I thanked my mother for that fear. I had watched her transform from a woman who had once colored her hours with fulfilling tasks into someone who withdrew into a brittle shell. Ten years ago, I'd been part of a literary community, in a graduate writing program, with writers who were my close friends. I'd worked for a well-known editor and writer. I'd taken classes. I'd published a novel.

As the months passed, I watched the other writers in the group find a direction. Vicki was toting in her early mother memories, such a tempting period to revisit, loaded with innocence and curiosity. Susan had been writing about her father, but it was her mother who needled at her. Joan had a tape, an interview with her mother. All of a sudden, I was jealous. How often had I tried to sit down with my mother and find out about her past, when suddenly she'd become distracted, or I'd become impatient?

I was the only one whose parents were divorced, and I began to think about this, especially when I listened to one of the other women read about how her mother had celebrated her father or tempered his outbursts. My mother, without my father, had turned into one restless spirit, and, as much as I was hesitant to write about her, I began to consider whether I might somehow rescue her from all those years of anguish. Shouldn't I try to recall all that she had once been and not just how she ended up? Ever since the other writers had summoned their mothers into the room, I could hear mine calling out to me, asking me to return to the beginning, when everything had seemed simpler. Here was my second chance.

El Día del Sombrero fashion show in San Juan; Lori,
right, with her mother and sister

Las Nereidas

That morning my mother and I didn't walk to school. We usually did, around eight, when the sun was calm. She'd hold my hand as we stepped in rhythm down the three blocks from our apartment building on Calle Joffre to the nursery school. I was four. My father drove my sister, who was in first grade, to the private elementary school ten minutes away.

The woman who ran the nursery school was bilingual, but I can't remember much else about her. I recall her tidy house and the freestanding arch through which the children, many of whom were American, passed every morning to enter the playground. Painted along the curve of the arch was the name *Las Nereidas*.

The concrete playground held a sandbox, a set of swings, a jungle gym, and, off in a corner, a shack. Inside were two or three picnic benches. There was no door, just a doorway. Palm trees, like lazy sentinels, surrounded the yard. What made me feel reflective, even at that age, was a flamboyan tree, the only stroke of brightness against the fronds and sky. The flowers were flaming red, and the branches blew like crimson scarves in the wind. When the flowers fell, they remained as a bold stain on the cement for several days.

I recall sipping from cold juice boxes that perspired in the humid air. The teacher must have fetched them from her kitchen while we ate our snacks, bowls of *platanos* and *chicharrones*. My mother packed me another snack, a bologna sandwich on white, no crust, in a small tin Flintstones lunchbox.

My mother, Estella Mae Webb, was born on July 4, 1924, in Tottenham, a region about six miles northeast of Charing Cross in Central London. She was mischievous, a pixie of a girl, often caned by the nuns at her Catholic school (her parents, Anglicans, advised her to think Catholic so she could attend the better school). After living through the Blitz, she boarded a ship to New York, where her older sister had settled.

Her sister's husband introduced my mother to my father, and after they were married, they moved to Puerto Rico. I was born on April 18, 1960, in Hato Rey. My father joined his two brothers, who had founded a chain of modern supermarkets called Pueblo. My mother seemed pleased to be known as Señora Milton Toppel. At a fashion show, the Spanish newspaper, *El Mundo*, asked her to pose with my sister and me for their style section. It was *El Día del Sombrero*, and my mother wore a hat she'd made, a flat basket filled with plastic fruits and little boxes of treats. The caption read: *"la señora de Milton Toppel lucio un tocado cómico."*

That morning, because of my new pink ballerina slippers that matched my leotard and tutu, my mother asked her chauffeur, Isabelo, to drive us to the nursery school. Isabelo was in his twenties, a shy, six-foot-tell black man with closely cropped hair and a chipped front tooth. Whenever I looked at him, I focused on his bright broken tooth. He didn't really speak English. I'd hear him at the front door, apologizing to my mother for something or other in his quick soft Spanish—he had scraped the car against a street lamp, or he was late because of a traffic jam.

My mother never learned to drive. She sometimes took a taxi, but a taxi required a fair grasp of Spanish, and hers was poor. When I was very young, I'd watch her try to communicate, having no idea that her lack of grace in a language I spoke so effortlessly was not an act. I thought she was trying to be funny.

With the air conditioner chilling the car, my mother draped a cotton cardigan around her shoulders; she wore a sleeveless linen dress that showed off her hourglass figure. Pink roses dotted the neckline, so our outfits complemented each another. The radio was playing local music, and her foot lightly tapped against the car floor.

My mother loved to dance but loved even more to watch my sister and me dance. She'd say, "Come on, Lol," and reach for my hand, her cigarette up in the air, her head tilted back, and she'd shimmy. I'd join in, laughing. Music was an affectionate animal that

131

leapt through the rooms of our home. We had a pianola, and we'd pop in a scroll for the keyboards to automatically play. My mother would sit between my sister and me, and we'd sing "Stella by Starlight," the keys rippling under our fearless fingers, our voices rising toward the end like a swaying choir. Her favorite songs were so ingrained in my mind that I felt I had written them. Sometimes she was the dreamer, like Judy Garland singing "Somewhere Over the Rainbow," other times the pragmatist, like Doris Day singing: "Que Sera, Sera."

Today was performance day. I had been practicing for some time.

"You look like a perfect little ballerina, Lollipop," my mother said. "You're not nervous, are you?"

I shook my head no, but I wasn't sure. I was fine at keeping my balance. The balance beam rose only a few inches off the ground, and it wasn't much longer than the sandbox.

Isabelo was perspiring at the back of his neck, although the air conditioner was blasting. I never considered that perhaps my mother was making him anxious.

"*Aquí, aquí,* Isabelo. And pick us up at *diez. Comprende?*" she said, signaling that he should not go any farther, as he'd almost missed the school.

Within seconds, he was holding the door for my mother, and she emerged like Queen Elizabeth, glancing around at her subjects. She had pride in her country's majesty and had taught my sister and me the British national anthem.

"Come, come, Lol," she said, flicking out her hand, and I grabbed it, eager to be a part of her beauty and eminence. "Oh, the cupcakes. Isabelo, *por favor.*"

Isabelo opened the passenger car door and lifted out a tray.

"*Yo tengo,*" she said, taking the tray from him. She always volunteered to bring in treats for the school. No longer holding her hand, I clutched the straw bag that hung over her shoulder.

As often as she played the frisky Brit who wished to partake in any festivity, she would sometimes pass through a mist of discontent, and I'd watch her closely and become too quiet. She'd notice right away and quickly excite me with an outing or a story.

We strolled through the archway and into the schoolyard, where a row of folding chairs had been set up under the shade of the flamboyan tree and in front of the balance beam. Drinks waited on the picnic tables inside the shack, its ceiling adorned with ribbons, and my mother and the nursery teacher chattered away while arranging the cupcakes on the tables. I stood in the doorway, staring at the balance beam. Next to it, a metal chair held a phonograph, and the teacher walked past me and stopped at the chair to greet everyone, pointing, at the same time, to where all the girls and boys should assemble. I scurried to my place. She lowered the needle on the record. I glanced at the row of mothers and spotted mine. Already smiling, she waved at me, but I looked away, embarrassed for having checked on her attentiveness.

The first girl began walking on the beam. She crossed to the end without ever once tilting off balance. Then the second girl; perhaps she was giggling. And then I was up. The beam seemed extremely narrow before I even touched it, as if overnight someone had cut its width in half. I stepped on the bar, spread out my arms, trying to look poised, as my mother had so often taught me, and I put one foot ahead of the other. While the music pushed me forward, I almost lost my balance. Fear surged through my body. I continued but, within seconds, tipped to the side. My foot struck the cement. I took off toward my mother and settled like a plume in her lap.

"Bravo! You did very well, Lori, very well. Did you hurt yourself?"

I didn't respond. I watched the next girl step up, while my mother rested my head against her shoulder, for I was, she knew, a lovely dancer.

Night & Day at the Beach

I wanted to be in the ocean, but I was stuck at the table, a grilled cheese, still warm, in front of me. I watched the waves breaking over the jetty.

"If you don't eat now, you'll be hungry before dinner," my mother said. Her wide-rimmed straw hat was flipped up at the front, revealing a round face with freckled cheeks. "And don't forget you have tennis at four with Nick."

I knew I'd have to wait at least twenty minutes before swimming. My mother had me convinced at the impressionable age of six that I'd drown if I even stood in water right after eating.

We were sitting at a table outside our cabana, one of many lined up at the top of a hill, each with its own square front yard. Down the hill, a concrete wall separated the cabanas from the beach. My sister, eight, was off with her best friend, drinking virgin piña coladas by the pool.

Our family had been going to the Caribe Hilton, one of the first hotels with a private beach club on the island, from the time I was born. After school, Isabelo would drive us the fifteen minutes from our apartment and then we'd trot through the open lobby as if it were ours. My sister and I learned to swim at the club; we learned to play tennis. On Fridays, my father sometimes left work early to join us.

After I'd waited long enough to digest my lunch, my mother took me to the pool instead of the beach. I didn't care; I just wanted to swim. I hopped into the water while my mother found a lounge chair. She had a famous pose, or that was how I saw it: she'd lie down on the lounge chair, bend her knees, slip one hand behind her head, angle her face toward the sun, sometimes wearing a hat, sometimes not. She wore those old-fashioned bathing suits without straps. Her hair, brownish-red, was short with straight bangs. She owned a variety of hats, which all shaded her creamy skin. Her fingers were sprinkled with rings.

I didn't have her complexion; I was as brown as topsoil.

"Can I have a quarter?" I asked her from the edge of the pool.

There she was in the lounge chair, alone, serene, holding a cigarette. If she had been with a girlfriend, she would have been talking nonstop, and I might have heard her say, "That Lori will crack her head open one of these days."

She fetched a quarter from her beach bag and flipped it to me. "No diving in the shallow end."

I slipped out and trotted over to the deep end, tossed the quarter, waited until it sank to the bottom, and dove to retrieve it. By now my mother was standing by the pool.

"Don't swim near the drain." Her hands were on her hips, and then she pointed toward the ladder. "Go on, throw it over there."

When it was time for tennis, we strolled back to the cabana. I showered while my mother tidied up, and then she, too, changed into a white tennis shirt and white shorts. Lisette, my sister, met us at the cabana, drinking a can of Tab. She and I shared certain facial expressions yet looked nothing alike. She was fair-skinned, blonde, and much more feminine than I.

"We're going to be late," she said.

My mother didn't have a lesson, but she told us that the tennis pro "fancied" her, so perhaps she'd hit with him afterwards.

"Your father doesn't care for Nick, but he's just jealous, that's all. Short men are, on the whole, insecure," she said.

When irritated with my father, she'd tell us he had a Napoleonic complex. Her complaints about his height made me wary of smaller men, and when I began dating, I gravitated toward the taller boys.

Nick Bollettieri was not much taller than my father, but he possessed that classic Italian look: dark-skinned with wavy black hair. He would become a famous tennis coach one day, although back then he was simply a young instructor who had a way with children. I remember he seemed fond of my mother and smiled while manipulating her hands on the racket. Was it a coincidence that handsome men became points on the circumference of her life? Our pediatrician was a charming, soft-spoken Puerto Rican who reminded her of Omar Sharif, our piano teacher an enthusiastic African-American who reminded her of Sidney Poitier.

After the lesson, Lisette and I browsed in the tennis shop, while my mother lingered on the court, drinking iced tea and talking over the net to Nick.

"I like this," I told my sister, holding up a light blue t-shirt.

"That's for a boy," she said, shutting her eyes in disbelief.

She had wonderful taste, I thought. She also had a beautiful forehand and was more at ease on the court than I. I tended to run too hard, swing too fast.

"Mommy, come on," my sister shouted.

On the way back to the cabana, my mother said, "I think Nick has a crush on me."

At the end of the day, I looked forward to rinsing off in the cabana shower, to the coolness of the concrete floor against my toes, and to the privacy of the small changing room outside the shower, where I could take my time dusting myself with baby powder. A Saks Fifth Avenue garment bag was hanging on a hook, holding our dresses and shoes.

We were going to eat at the hotel, at The Rotisserie, my favorite restaurant. My mother wore a long strapless dress, a strand of pearls around her neck, and her hair, adorned with a hairpiece, was swept into a beehive, prepared by the hotel beautician.

The Rotisserie was up a flight of stairs. At the bottom of the stairs, a small pond cradled what seemed like the same goldfish for as long as I could remember. Sometimes while we waited for our dinner to come, my sister and I would take a piece of bread from the table, gallop down the stairs, and feed the fish. I liked to imagine hiding inside the restaurant after hours, waltzing around the tables, taking cake and ice cream from the kitchen.

My father had his table, the one near the window, with a view of the ocean, its waves shimmering in the beams of the beach floodlights. He began the evening by ordering wine.

"Stella, red or white tonight?"

"Red. But don't get that red we had last time. I didn't care for it."

He picked a different bottle. The wine steward trotted away, the shiny silver cup a swinging pendulum around his neck. The cup, my father explained, was just for show at the restaurant, but, once upon a time, the sommelier had used it to taste and assess the wine. My father's expertise always made more of an impression on me than on my mother.

Upon returning, the wine steward let my father taste the wine, and my father let my mother taste it.

"Now that is lovely." She flashed a smile.

My mother then waved over one of the musicians who was drifting from table to table and requested her favorite song. She embarrassed us by insisting we also give a request. We blushed. Giggled. Said nothing.

Men were entranced by her innate musicality, the lowering of a shoulder before she spoke, the batting of her eyes while saying thank you, the perfectly-timed flirtatious kick, forcing her gown to slip away and reveal her slender white calf and ankle. Whenever we were at family parties, she and my father would dance. Her steps were fluid, while my father bounced up and down, sometimes singing under his breath, "Bee-dee-wee-dee-ho."

The trio played my mother's song, "Bésame Mucho," the necks of the guitars bowing to the table, and my father ordered a Caesar salad, prepared tableside.

"Add a bit more cheese; it's so much better with a bit more cheese," my mother said, smiling, and the waiter grinned, grating the cheese with fervor.

One of my father's best friends ate there often, a man who had never married. He owned a circus that had something to do with Barnum & Bailey, and I loved his laugh, a rumble that rolled across a room and made his belly jiggle. Perhaps he sailed over to our table that evening, accompanied by another gentleman (he was never with a woman).

"How's life, my friend?" my father might ask.

My mother didn't particularly care for the man. Over time she began to dislike many of my father's friends; they were too jolly, too self-indulgent. My father, forever loquacious around others, seemed, at times, snuffed out by my mother when alone with her.

We, as children, were the primary source of her infectious spirit. She would have been content to keep us around as much as possible, even when all our friends were being sent away to summer camp. My father, loyal to the customs and traditions of families in what he liked to call "our social standing," wanted us to be real campers, on our own for two months. Independence, at any age, he believed, was admirable. My mother had finally agreed to allow us to go to a day camp outside of New York City for a few weeks that coming June. Our family would stay at the company's apartment in The Hampshire House hotel on Central Park South. She made it clear that sleep-away camp, at our age, was out of the question.

At some point in the evening, she must have been thinking about those summer hours when she would be without us, as she said, "You're lucky. When I was little, there were no camps with the war going on." She often spoke of bomb shelters, air raids, and food rations, as if they were recollections from a pleasant family outing. At age six, I didn't pay much attention to any of that talk, and I wasn't at all nervous about the summer. Day camp would be a breeze. I'd come home to my mother.

My sister and I were restless between courses. I emptied the melted wax from inside one candleholder to mold into a rabbit, and Lisette did the same with the other candleholder to shape a duck.

"You're making a mess, girls. Jesus Christ, what am I going to do with you two?" my father said, not at all angry yet shaking his head and brushing the wax remnants into his hand to toss into the ashtray.

"Do you want the *profiteroles*, Lori?" my mother asked, placing the menu over her chest like a fan. She knew I loved the little puffs of pastry filled with ice cream. My sister ordered the baked Alaska.

The waiter sounded apologetic. "Mrs. Toppel, you know you have to order the baked Alaska a few minutes before. A little time it will take."

"Please see what you can do for us, Rafael. It's so delicious"

"He can't make it come out any faster if it's not ready. Unless you want a piece of junk, the best food takes a little time to–"

"Prepare. We know, Daddy," my sister finished for him, rolling her eyes.

In a matter of ten minutes, the waiter reappeared at our table with my sister's dessert. He touched a match to the white icing and a circle of flame crowned the cake.

"See, girls, if you don't ask, you won't get," my mother said, smiling at the waiter.

Terrace with a Zoo

A lean man in oversized pants was perched on a stool outside the entrance of Plaza Las Americas, the shopping center where we often bought clothes. His hand rested on a supermarket cart filled with chicks, their feathers dyed in bright Easter colors. I peered through the bars of the cart at the mound of squirming chicks, and my sister and I begged our mother for one.

Bending over the cart to examine them more closely, my mother said, "I suppose the pink one's cute."

"Oh, I love pink," Lisette said, and for a dollar, we took home a chick. I was, at the most, five years old.

My mother allowed the chick to trot around the house, in spite of the fact that she'd later find a trail of white splats on the floor, and when Pinky began resembling an adult chicken and was no longer pink, she, without hesitation, gave it away to the superintendent of the building.

Having realized she should have never let the chick roam free, my mother warned us about our next pets: "You can't let the bunnies hop around inside." We named the rabbits Melissa and Buttons and covered the bottom of their cage with cedar shavings. We set the cage on the terrace, and the bunnies had their own view of Old San Juan and the ocean. I fed carrots and lettuce to the rabbits, while our housekeeper, an animated Peruvian woman, Maria, cleaned the cage and joked that she'd like to take one home for a stew. When Buttons bit me on the hand, I said nothing, but when he drew blood from my sister's finger, she told my mother who instantly offered the pair to our neighbor.

Soon enough, we were given a parakeet, but it died within the week. My mother replaced it with another, and when that one perished, we gave up on parakeets. She then bought us canaries, luminous songbirds, and their whistling was sweet and constant. I forget what their fate was, but the list of pets living on our terrace is written on my memory—turtles, mice, hamsters, hermit crabs, and lizards, each creature staying only a short while. My mother's immediate refilling of each pet's space was a clever trick; how little time we had to miss the old one.

She never cared for cats. Cats were the witch's familiar, and her fear was proof of how much she believed in the supernatural. She was entranced with the idea of spells and curses, often assuring us that if anyone did our family wrong, she'd cast a spell on that person. The legend of Dracula was one of her favorites, and she collected as many vampire books as she could find.

I remember how she'd crack my bedroom door open, deepen her voice, and warn me, "I've come to suck your blood." I'd look up at her, half surprised, half scared, and she'd stand there, waiting for me to speak, and then burst into laughter.

On some nights, particularly if she and I had watched one of her favorite vampire movies on television, Bela Lugosi as the Count, I'd place a cross on my night table before I went to sleep. My father was Jewish, and my mother, having converted (for some reason I never quite believed that she had, but my father vouched on her behalf), was content to raise her daughters as Jews. With no real crosses to be found, I made one out of two pencils and a rubber band.

In spite of her superstitions, somehow we ended up with a cat, a Siamese male, a specimen of unrepentant elegance that would pad along the arms of the den couch. Unlike all the other pets, the cat was forbidden on the terrace, as he could slip through the bars and plummet down twelve stories. One day, in spite of all our caution, someone left the terrace door open.

"I'm so sorry," my mother told me when I came home from school.

Whose fault was it? I must have wondered. How could someone have acted so carelessly?

Later I overheard my mother tell my father that the superintendent had found the dead cat near the pool. She'd been right: cats were just trouble.

When our apartment was robbed later that year, my father had a carpenter install a floor-to-ceiling wrought iron gate at the front door, but that wasn't enough security for my mother. In no time, Petey, a miniature schnauzer, became guardian of our household, my mother's idea of a watchdog. I fell in love with him.

One day I was in my room, playing with my favorite paper dolls. I was seven. A few weeks earlier, Petey had been swept away to spend the weekend at a farm, as my father had agreed to have him sire another schnauzer. My parents promised me that we could adopt one of the puppies. I could hear my sister telling my father outside my bedroom how disappointed I'd be that the female dog hadn't become pregnant. I remember being touched by my sister's concern, and when she gave me the news, I acted more upset than I actually felt. That night my mother tried to lighten my mood by suggesting we get another puppy. Soon enough, we had two-month-old Poco, another male miniature schnauzer.

My sister and I lavished our attention on the dogs, and, at times, our mother joined us. For Petey's birthday, she made a heart-shaped hamburger and served it to him on a fancy white plate. She said that she thought Petey was jealous of the puppy, so he deserved a special treat. We sang happy birthday to him, while I pretended to play the pianola.

When we moved to New York, we were told we had to give away the dogs. I must have protested and cried, but I was not surprised.

Many years later, in our New York City apartment, I joined my mother in the kitchen one afternoon. She was making tea. I was peering into the fridge, looking for a snack and hoping to avoid conversation. I was a teenager. I had my own Yorkshire terrier, and my sister had a toy poodle.

My mother often had to remind me to walk the dog, who was always at my feet, and perhaps I began petting it. Warming one hand over the cup of steaming tea, my mother told me, "I hated all those pets you and Lisette had as kids, but I could never say no to you. Your faces used to light up every time you touched a rabbit, a dog, whatever had fur." She chuckled. "But I'll never forget that bloody chicken, and how you wanted to keep it, even though it was getting bigger and bigger. If my father had been around, he'd have cut its head off and cooked it up for dinner. Chickens can walk around headless, you know." Then she made a face as if she'd tasted a rotten fruit, and added that, in spite of her disgust, she always ate what she'd been given as a child. She resumed sipping her tea, and when I didn't respond, said, "That's just how it was when I was a little girl, and I had a very happy childhood."

The Sisters from England

How happy was my mother's childhood? She came from a big family, two girls and four boys, and grew up in what I imagine was a gritty suburb. Her father earned his living as a furniture polisher, and on the weekends he played his music at a nearby club, a horn of some kind, a trumpet or a sax. He liked to box, she told me. My mother loved to spew out her disconnected remembrances, repeating some more frequently than others: her family had an icebox, not a fridge; her father built a bomb shelter in the basement; her father's name was Oliver, her mother called him Ollie; he died when she was only twelve; she had an older brother, no longer alive, whom she disliked intensely; he tried to steal some of her mother's money after she was widowed; and her mother had the prettiest red hair that fell to her waist.

(My father told me he was sure my grandfather hit his kids, especially my mother, who couldn't sit still. I never asked him how he knew this. I must have assumed my mother had confided in him.)

My grandfather nicknamed my mother the "little bugger." She was the younger sister, the tomboy, the one always stirring up trouble. Eileen, her sister, was the "goodie-good," the one my grandfather favored, the beauty of the family, and when my mother left England a few years after the war, it was to follow Eileen, who had married an American and settled in Queens, New York.

After my aunt gave birth to fraternal twins, my mother moved in with her to help with the babies. She supported herself by working at a textile factory. About my cousins, my mother liked to say, "I'm the one who took care of them. I changed their diapers and played with them whenever I could." She adored them, she'd add; she never minded.

A few years later, my uncle introduced her to my father, whom she married at the Plaza Hotel in Manhattan in 1957. My father, born in 1919 and raised in Franklin, New Jersey, was adventurous, personable, and he carried my mother away to San Juan to partner with his brothers in their supermarket venture. How romantic, my mother must have thought, but, in time, she made it clear that if there was any romance on the humid island, she couldn't find it. She despised the heat, had difficulty learning Spanish, and, perhaps most of all, she missed her sister.

On occasion, my aunt and her family visited, and we'd spend the weekend at the Dorado Beach Hotel, a country club an hour outside of San Juan. Our rooms were next to one another, the beach a few steps away. I remember my aunt lying in a chair, silent under a palm tree, her eyes behind large sunglasses. She'd read, lifting her head every now and again to smile at me as I played on the beach

My mother and aunt looked alike. Both had the same straight nose, high cheekbones, smooth complexion, and auburn hair, but my mother was small and outspoken. My aunt was taller, refined, and reserved. Although I thought my mother was pretty, even illuminated somehow, I always saw my aunt as the stunning, poised figure in the background. She had a wonderful smile and eyes that pulled you in.

When we visited her in New York, we'd stay at the apartment in the Hampshire House, and I can remember Eileen in that room, although she is silent. My mother is asking her if she'd like something to drink, and soon they're both drifting out the door, dressed in their long leather gloves and fur coats, on their way to dinner, walking ahead of their husbands.

On weekends, we'd drive to my aunt's house in Floral Park, where my mother and aunt would retreat to the kitchen. They were like two canaries, in flight around each other, whistling out their stories. My mother would sit at my aunt's kitchen table, waving her cigarette in the air, telling about her morning. She'd then jump up, flit about the kitchen in her fitted black pants and turtleneck sweater, the heels of her black pumps clicking against the tile, and my aunt would heat the kettle for tea. There was jam in a saucer, toast with butter on a platter. There was a small round table near the windows. The house was quaint, the yard just big enough to hold a few chairs and a grill. My aunt's voice grew in my mother's presence. They comforted each other with what sounded to me like an avalanche of words, one sister's phrase bumping up against the other's: "Stel, did I tell you 'bout Loretta…" "Well Peter knows and she didn't even mention the weekend…" "Or bother to phone…" "Fancy another?… "

When I was ten, we moved to New York. My parents bought a resplendent apartment in the United Nations Plaza, a duplex with a view of the river and the East Side, very different from my aunt's modest house. My mother hired an interior designer, and with her discerning eye, she helped him create a distinct palette in every room. The dining room had an early nineteenth-century tapestry on the wall depicting the English countryside, a picnic scene by a river. She shared her good fortune by sending dollops of cash as birthday gifts to all her nieces and nephews. The apartment was sprawling, tasteful, and immaculate, yet my recollections of our seven years there are dimmed by despair and discord. In place of the pianola, there was a gleaming baby grand, and no one played it.

We kept the apartment in San Juan. My father stayed there whenever he flew down for business. He missed the island. I knew that. Although he was now in charge of a new chain of wholesale supermarkets on Long Island, he'd moan about the long commute every morning.

I don't recall seeing much of my aunt during those years. She must have been slipping in and out of poor health. She still talked to my mother frequently on the phone. My mother never criticized her, and as much as she liked my uncle, she'd blame him if my aunt became despondent or withdrawn, admonishing him for bringing home his poker buddies, a boisterous crew who interfered with Eileen's much-needed rest.

Although my father was friendly with my uncle, he was never that comfortable with Eileen. He talked to my sister and me sometimes about it, as if he were simply perplexed by her behavior. She was too tough on my uncle. She sometimes acted a bit nutty. He viewed my aunt's peculiarities, I'm sure, as an extension of my mother's own troubling side.

After two years in the city, I was diagnosed with severe colitis and missed several weeks of school. One day my mother told me my aunt had gone to church to light a candle for me. I was surprised and honored by her act of piety, and when my aunt decided to visit me, which was unusual, since she, like my mother, didn't drive, both my mother and I were extremely pleased.

My aunt offered to make me lunch. With that, a tone was set, my aunt at the stove, and my mother seated, telling her where everything was. I remember listening and admiring my aunt's calm while she cooked, and I noted how much more at ease my mother was, how glad she was to have her sister helping her.

Our kitchen had custom mahogany cabinets and a back staircase leading to the housekeeper's room. I wonder if my mother ever felt gratified that she had acquired the nicer home, that, for once, she was ahead of her sister, that someone, somehow, was favoring her. While I savored my lunch and looked out the window at the skyscrapers and the East River, my mother told my aunt about all the doctors I had seen. Hearing my mother unload her concerns, I felt lucky to be her daughter. I had no doubt she would always do all that she could for me.

A month before my fifteenth birthday we flew down to San Juan for our school break. One afternoon the phone rang. Within seconds of answering, my mother screamed and doubled over. She was heaving, pressing the receiver against her thigh. My father took the phone from her hand. After saying a few words, he hung up and embraced her. They hardly ever hugged each other, and I think now that he was actually holding her up. Eileen had died.

That evening, my mother, no longer crying, sat at the edge of my bed and told me my Aunt Eileen had been suffering from cancer. "The pain killed her," she said.

I knew my aunt had been sick. In the morning, however, my father told my sister and me that she had taken an overdose of pills. We were in the car, but I've no memory as to where we were headed. "She had a history of mental instability; this wasn't her first attempt at trying to hurt herself. But she meant business this time." My father explained that after taking the pills, she had tied a plastic bag over her head. He didn't sound cruel or harsh, and, if anything, he seemed somewhat exasperated, as if he had felt this coming and wasn't sure now what to do.

Years later, I'd learn just how delicate my aunt was, how she had suffered from hysterical fits, and had even been taken, in an emergency, to the psychiatric clinic at Bellevue hospital. But that day, in the car, I sat picturing my aunt in her bed, supine, graceful, with a clear veil over her face, and I kept in just how shaken I was.

When her two brothers from England flew over for the funeral, they gathered in our living room with relatives who lived nearby. We never used the living room; it was a showcase for my mother's antiques—cigar cutters, crystal vases, nude statues, a pair of white silk sofas, and the baby grand—and I listened as the voices from my mother's past gradually shed their sorrowful tone. I listened to the short bursts of laughter followed by the natural banter between her brothers.

My mother ordered our housekeeper (Maria's sister, who had been such a part of our life in Puerto Rico) to bring in more drinks and food. She tried to smile at her family, dipping her shoulder toward her brothers in response to their requests, as if she were an actor who had momentarily forgotten how her character should move.

After everyone left, I watched her weep. She didn't care how loud she was. She then stared at the walls, limp and dazed. For months, a perpetual sadness seemed to pursue her, a purity of emotion, and I imagined she felt somewhat responsible, as if she had failed to sustain her sister's joy and hope. She hadn't counted on her sister going anywhere without her, and, this time, it was impossible for my mother to follow.

33rd Floor

My mother walked into my bedroom carrying a tray with a cup of tea and a plate of toast and jam. Her gait was purposeful, and she set down the tray to feel my head.

The walls were too bold: orange and yellow tulips with apple green leaves printed on a satin-like fabric. I had once loved the big flowers surrounding me, but recently I'd been at home so much that the apartment had become my text to criticize.

I read poetry while in bed: Rimbaud's *Illuminations*, Baudelaire's *Fleurs du Mal.* My Yorkshire terrier slept beside my hip. On the night table sat my phone and an ever-present glass of water. I had a television, a stereo, a built-in desk and bookshelves, my own bathroom.

"Put something little in your stomach. See if you can keep this down."

"I want to shower." She forbade me to shower when I was sick; I had to use dry shampoo.

I bit into the toast. "Lisette is bringing home my homework?"

"Yes, I spoke to your English teacher. She said not to worry."

Worry wasn't the word; I was stricken over all the school I'd missed.

She sat down on my bed and neatened the covers, assuring me I could make up my work.

Although visibly tired, my mother was always well groomed, her auburn hair shining. She had gone to the beauty parlor that morning. At forty-eight, she was still slender with smooth skin; her hands were exquisite with delicate fingers, long pink-painted nails. She never did any hard housework, no task that would mark her hands.

Manhattan was warming up—all winter coats had been stored away—and tulips and daffodils painted the sidewalks of Park Avenue. Whenever I thought I was well enough to leave my bed,

I'd go to class and then relapse the next day. My friends called me, but they didn't understand the disease, and neither did I. For almost a year, I'd been pumped with steroids, and although I was thin, my face was swollen.

"It's psychosomatic," one doctor had said, and my mother dismissed him. He recommended a psychiatrist, to whom I told a bunch of lies, and after a couple of visits, my mother said I'd had enough. She then proceeded to take me to three or four more doctors before the fifth, the kindest, offered the correct diagnosis. My father accompanied us from time to time, but when he did, he was often detached, asking a few questions, seemingly encouraged by the responses. My mother explained all my symptoms to the doctor in detail, carrying a little black notebook in her purse in which she wrote the names of all my medications, any tests done, and every one of my reactions. She wore dark slacks and a silk blouse like Katherine Hepburn.

She was my nurse; that was her choice, and she wouldn't have changed it for anything. When one doctor suggested I be hospitalized for a series of tests, she refused. She could take care of me at home and bring me in for the tests. We watched cartoons, movies, and documentaries; we read poetry and novels. We ate together. Every now and then the symbiotic nest we had composed was invaded by the truth: she was at a breaking point with my father.

"Your father will be home soon." My mother was cleaning my night table of used tissues. I had eaten some of the toast and could smell the roast beef our housekeeper, Emperatriz, was cooking.

After my mother left, I slipped into the bathroom and undressed. I knew the ritual. No shower, no bath; my mother was afraid I'd catch a chill. I cleaned myself with a washcloth, and then sprayed the too-fragrant dry shampoo on my hair. It was a powdery substance. I fluffed up my hair, brushed it, and stared at myself. I got back into bed.

When my father came home, he entered my room with a knock. He kissed me. A short man with heavy glasses, wearing a grey suit, he was soft-spoken and liked to laugh, although he hadn't done much of that lately. He sat at the edge of my bed, folded his hands on his lap.

"The principal called. They're concerned you might not pass into eighth grade. By law there are a number of days you have to be in school."

I was about to cry when my mother stepped in. "What are you telling her?"

"Stella, she has to know."

"What if I pass my finals, Daddy? Will I be all right?"

"You should try," my father said, taking my hand. "I'm going to take a bath." He drifted out of the room with his head down.

I swore to myself I'd be at school on Friday and get through my tests, no matter what. I'd already missed one or two exams, so I asked my mother to call and make sure I could make up those as well.

On the way to school, in the taxi, my mother lit up a cigarette.
"You should quit," I said.

"These are so low in nicotine, it doesn't count as smoking." She glanced out the window, inhaling the smoke.

I took four finals in a row with my mother in the room. Why was she there? I could excuse myself to go to the bathroom, more than once if needed, and my mother would nod knowingly to my teacher. I could ask for water–dehydration was always a threat. My mother was a rescue boat, and I didn't think I had the courage, after all the pain I'd experienced with the initial stage of the disease, to get through the hours without her.

She sat and read a novel, perhaps. She sat and doodled, perhaps; she was an avid doodler. She sat and watched me, glancing at her daily planner every few minutes. Yes, she was there, in her navy blue pants suit, with her matching lizard purse, waiting to avert the next crisis.

I passed every test. Eighth grade was on the horizon, after all.

One evening, from the kitchen, I overheard my father talking to my mother in the dining room. As always, he was sitting at the head of the table, my mother to his right. My sister and I had already eaten on folding tables in the den, watching *The Partridge Family*, and now I was keeping Emperatriz company while she prepared dinner for my parents.

I remember her economy of movement; from one spot she could do so much: chop, clean, organize. She was a stout woman, with short arms and legs, and hair as glossy as a crow's feathers. Smiling, she told me not to eavesdrop on my parents.

My father was telling my mother he wasn't interested in what the maid had done wrong.

My mother accused him of never being interested. "I'm the one who keeps the house clean and running, while our daughter is very sick at home."

"I've had a long week, Stella."

Then she taunted him. I remember that taunting too well. She'd remind him that his brother wasn't happy with the stores in Long Island, and how afraid he was of this brother, the head of the company.

"I told you we should start talking to a lawyer."

"Yes, take the easy way out, Milton, you always do."

Was it then I burst into the room, in my pajamas, unusually energetic?

I sat to my father's left, moving the chair closer to his. I studied the tapestry, noting how all the wild animals had gathered by the river near the picnicking women. It was a peaceful scene.

"Do you want to play backgammon later?"

"Maybe. But for now," he said, becoming perkier, "I think I'll get that new cognac out of…"

"I'll get it for you."

I hurried through the kitchen and into the hall that contained his wine cellar, a large closet with built-in racks, a thermometer, and a row of wood cabinets. I grabbed the bottle of cognac and leaned against the cabinets, taking in the smell of the cedar. I brought him the bottle and followed him into the den where he fetched a glass. My father poured himself a little cognac and then settled down in his reading chair with the paper.

"Let me read the newspaper, baby. Come on, bug off." He lifted his glasses and sped through the articles, flipping the pages within seconds. He would always ask me to bug off when it came to his catching up on the news.

I headed for my sister's bedroom. She was listening to a Minnie Ripperton record. Lisette's room was a golden yellow, the wallpaper dotted with an array of black-eyed Susans. It was a warmer room, I thought, more mature than mine, and I plopped down on her bed. Her hair was wheat-colored, striped with blonde highlights. She wore wedges, her stylish stilts. Having lost the weight that had burdened her when she'd been seven or eight, she was now notably thin.

I asked, "Do you still like Gil?"

"He's so cute, isn't he? Peggy's going to the senior prom with Mark."

My sister filled me in on the gossip. I admired her, and all that she represented—defiance *and* fashion. She talked back to my mother; she wasn't afraid. Earlier that week she had warned my mother that all her fighting with my father was making me feel worse. She was repeating what I'd said to her, as I knew she'd pass it on to my mother, forcing them to behave themselves, if only for a few days.

My mother threw open the door. "Go to bed, Lori." She'd become wired with anger. I knew it had nothing to do with my being up late.

"I'm not tired."

"You're sick," she shouted. "Haven't you already missed countless days of school?"

My sister told me to go to bed. She glared at my mother.

I got into bed, and after my mother turned out the lights, I picked up the remote control and turned on the television, keeping the volume low.

Was that one of the evenings my father tiptoed into my room around midnight, after I'd finally fallen asleep? He got into the other twin bed and started to snore. He always woke me.

I'd lie there, thinking that he was going to leave us. Sometimes I'd get up and draw back the curtain to look at the city lights. My father had given me the telescope from our terrace in San Juan, which he had used to watch the cruise ships. I zoomed in on a living room in the building across the street and watched a silhouette move around, and then I got back in bed, wondering about someone else's night.

My father moved out a year later, returning to our San Juan apartment. He filed for divorce, suing my mother on the grounds of mental cruelty, and he began dating. My mother took old photographs of my father and scratched out his face with the points of a scissors. She screamed at my sister and me over small mishaps. She relied on tranquilizers. She repeatedly insulted my father whenever we were around, and I was quick to peg her as the instigator. I later found photocopies of her letters to her lawyer, in which she wrote that I was rebellious, angry, and that my father was manipulating me.

Over the next eight years, my parents would move in and out of different courtrooms, some in New York, some in Puerto Rico. In high school, with my illness finally in remission. I skipped a grade. I was already in the highest levels of English, Spanish, and math, so it wasn't hard to do. I had to get out of my house.

One night I was standing at the window in the den, dazed from having finished a long school project, when my mother walked in. I was sixteen.

"Your father's dating a whore. All she wants is his money. But it's my bloody money, not hers."

I said nothing.

"He's no fucking angel," she said and left for the kitchen, where I could hear her shouting at the new housekeeper.

She had fired Emperatriz, dismissed her without a second thought, after Emperatriz had physically blocked me from my mother's wrath. As much as I missed her, I was relieved she had been freed.

Another night, I remember walking into my mother's bathroom, where she was sitting on her vanity seat. She was in a robe, smoking a cigarette and crying, half-turned toward the mirror over the sink. She wasn't looking at herself.

"I just can't do it anymore. I can't fight him. Why won't he just give me what I need?"

Her robe was open, and I saw her white underwear against her pale skin.

"Why don't you guys stop with all of it?"

"Tell him to stop," she snapped.

I stepped out.

Then on another night, when she asked for my reassurance, I didn't recognize her need. I was rummaging through the fridge, thinking of a boy I liked. She was at the stove, dipping a tea bag in and out of a cup.

"Why don't we go away, just you and me, Lol? I don't know. Maybe to England."

"When would we do that?"

"Maybe Christmas. We could be with my family. Wouldn't it be nice to be with family over the holidays?"

By now she was suffering. I didn't see it. All I saw was her rage bouncing off everything, especially me.

I probably said, "Yes, that'd be nice," as I took out the orange juice.

In the den of the United Nations apartment

My Boys Are Hers

It was a Sunday, early spring. Edith Piaf was playing on the stereo. Music, snacks on the table, sometimes even presents. Whenever I arrived at my mother's apartment, I felt as if she were expecting company and not her daughter. The sunlight filtered through the half-drawn blinds, the apartment immaculate. I could almost count the few dust particles suspended in the streams of light.

My husband and I lived in Boca Raton, Florida, but we were in Manhattan for a close friend's wedding. We were going to leave our sons, sixteen-month-old twins, with my mother for the first time. Nelly, the woman who helped me, was there to help her.

Like Maria and Emperatriz, Nelly was Peruvian. But they were from a small town in the north, and Nelly was from Lima. She was educated, intuitive, and serene, and had four children of her own. She didn't believe in raising her voice. She was like a hands-on grandmother to my sons. Nelly and I would take walks with the boys by the ocean and she'd point to the water, tell them its name, and I repeated it, too. I loved the Spanish language and how gently she delivered it to my sons. I loved how their first word, after mommy and papa, was *agua*.

"The boys are gorgeous," my mother said. "They look British. They have those rosy cheeks and smooth complexions. Put the stroller in the living room. Will they sleep in it?"

"Yes," I said, as I watched my sons begin to doze off, strapped in the double stroller that I had somehow maneuvered through the door and into the living room. Her taste was still traditional and clean, and she had bought all new furniture after having to sell the U.N. apartment. She had a long white sofa, a custom mahogany armoire, and a white rug printed with bold geometric shapes. My boys were a handful, constantly moving and grazing everything with their fingers. Their long blond hair was supple, like a new leaf, their eyes green.

My mother had gained a considerable amount of weight. She adjusted her clothes to fit her altered frame in the most fashionable way she knew. She wore long sweaters over narrow-legged cotton pants with an elastic waist. Although seventy, she still colored her hair reddish-brown and on occasion flashed the same wide smile I remembered as a child. She hardly wore makeup anymore, complaining she was allergic to too many things.

On the dining room table, she had left a cigarette burning in an ashtray, and so she scuttled over to extinguish it. She wasn't at all content living in this nicely appointed two-bedroom. She was lonely, obsessed with her health and housekeepers, and had become faithful to her sedatives at night. My father had remarried; his new wife was twenty years younger than he.

For the moment, however, my mother was willing to succumb to delight, and the energy that had once made her shine in Puerto Rico emerged again. It was contagious. Both boys had pacifiers in their mouths. Alex's fell out as his head slipped to the side while he slept. His sudden movement alerted Ben, who suddenly awakened and began to cry. Alex's eyes popped open, and he started to whimper. I picked him up, while Nelly took Ben, and my mother hurried into her bedroom and returned with a large wooden jewelry box and a traveling jewelry case.

"Who wants to play pirates?" she said, placing the box and case on the coffee table.

Nelly removed the Steuben glass snail and a brass sculpture of an archer from the table.

"Oh, don't worry about those, Nelly. Let them play," my mother told her and extracted a long strand of pearls from the jewelry box.

She took out her treasures one by one, all costume jewelry, all products of one of my mother's recent obsessions: purchasing off the QVC channel copies of the real jewels she had once worn. After the divorce proceedings had begun, she claimed my father wasn't giving her enough money, and so she sold all her jewelry, her pear-shaped wedding ring, her diamond necklace, even a tiara, all prizes from another era, which I can still picture today.

Her taste remained elegant; her desperation and sadness couldn't fool her eye. The pearls were not so shiny as to look fake; the gold chains were fragile; the earrings were clip-ons, with glass emeralds at their center. The boys, now sitting on the rug, giggled as my mother tied scarves around their heads like pirates' bandannas. She draped the strands of pearls around Ben's neck and gave Alex earrings. They bolted over to the box and picked up different trinkets. My mother then attached the clip-on earrings to their shirts and hooked silver chains around their waists. Nelly and I made sure anything small stayed where we could see it.

"You're a frightening bloke," my mother said to Ben. "Which one's this?" she asked, double-checking.

"Ben," I said. "His eyes are different."

"I could eat you up," she said, kissing Ben's plump hand. He smiled and then handed her a bracelet, and she repeatedly thanked him.

She hurried over to the entranceway, where, in a corner, a ceramic stand held several umbrellas and a few canes. Whenever she left home, she took a cane with her. Her feet hurt; she had constant vertigo. I had seen her cross a street as the "Don't Walk" sign began to blink, and she'd wave her cane around to stop the cars.

She slipped the cane between her legs and steered it like a horse over to Alex. "Okay, giddy-up, we're off."

The game went on until, out of sheer exhaustion, the two boys begged me for their pacifiers and collapsed on the floor, curled up, and fell asleep. My puppies, I called them.

I felt comfortable leaving them now. My husband, Doug, was meeting me at the hotel where the wedding was to take place.

"Do you need money for a taxi? Here, take this so you don't have to hunt in your purse. And don't worry about the boys."

I accepted the twenty-dollar bill, thanked her, and told her I'd call. I kissed her quickly. She didn't hug often; she didn't show me the kind of affection she had once shown me as a child. Now any gestures of love were reserved for her grandsons.

"Nelly will put them on the bed in a few minutes. Leave their pacifiers in; otherwise, they may wake up," I said.

"Stop worrying. Have fun. I'll feed them when they wake up. I made spaghetti and meatballs."

When I called an hour later, they were still asleep on the floor. "I put blankets on top of them and soft pillows under their heads. They're like two angels. I told Nelly to leave them there, so they don't wake up."

"Thanks, Mommy."

"Oh, and you really should get them off those pacifiers, Lori, for the simple reason that they're bad for their teeth. I never used them with you or Lisette."

"I will. They're still young."

"Well, I took them right out of their mouths after you left and, wouldn't you know, they stayed sound asleep."

Lori's mother with her twin grandsons

A Warm Bath

My mother announced she was selling her apartment. This was unexpected. She had lived there for over twelve years. The idea came about through my sister, who had studied our mother's financial portfolio statement one day and told her she needed more cash in her account. My sister didn't visit often, although she lived in the city, but whenever she paid attention to my mother, she did so in a loving manner and investigated some facet of her existence with a thorough eye, so my mother felt both delighted and eager to act on any of her suggestions.

My mother's home, given her age–she was seventy-five–was a hallowed place where convenience glittered at her fingertips. My sister didn't think about that. I didn't think about that.

I thought that, perhaps, my mother would be happier if she lived closer to me. I was in northern Westchester County, and perhaps a change would be just what she needed. Her health was deteriorating. Her pain was chronic–her back, her hands, her head– and her muscles had almost atrophied, so that her calves were thin, while her thighs and mid-section were plush with flesh.

The apartment sold remarkably fast.

She took a room at the Sutton Hotel, a few blocks from where she used to live, but she couldn't stay there long, so I invited her to stay with us. We went apartment hunting in Stamford, Connecticut, fifteen minutes from my home. I suggested she look for a house to rent, and perhaps Nelly would want to live with her. Instead, my mother decided to take a two-bedroom apartment in a doorman building. It was an older apartment but the least expensive of all the places we had seen, and not my favorite. She wanted to make the point that she was concerned about money, in keeping with why she had sold her home in the first place. She had overreacted, I told myself. Yes, maybe she'd have to refinance her mortgage, or set up a reasonable budget, but instead she had panicked. After having signed the contract, she had called me and said calmly, "I don't think I should move, Lol. I made a mistake. Would you see if you could get me out of this?" I couldn't.

Given her impetuousness, should I have been more patient and perhaps illuminated the advantages of the newer apartments in Stamford, and encouraged her to keep looking? I was too tired. Driving her from place to place, making sure she was eating, running errands for her, I was so relieved she had finally found somewhere suitable, or, at the least, had settled on the illusion of suitability, that I gave in. She was scheduled to move to Stamford in two weeks.

At my house, her mood leapt all over the place. The bed wasn't comfortable, and why didn't I paint the den a brighter color?

One morning, Alex woke up with a high fever. He was six. I cooled him down by dabbing his forehead and wrists with a damp cloth.

"That feels good," he told me, and I knew how good it felt. My mother had performed the same ritual on me as a child.

Later he walked downstairs where she sat at the kitchen counter. Her loose clothing billowed down to her knees, and I knew she couldn't stand to look at herself.

"What shall we play?" she asked Alex. Her hair was set in rollers under a net, and Nelly had been scheduled to brush it out.

"Play?" he said, standing near me. "Like a game?"

Soon they were in the living room, and he was explaining to her the rules of "Don't Wake Daddy," and he was smiling, and now he was climbing on top of the table to get within inches of her.

"Oh, dear, I'm not much good at this, Alexander, for the simple reason that you're a lucky little bugger."

That night, while I was putting him to bed, he said, "Nanny's really nice."

A few nights later, as we were all going out for pizza, she said, "This is the first time I've felt like I have a family."

In a few days, she was moving out.

Nelly, Doug, and I had set up the new apartment. I asked my mother what I should do with the furniture that didn't fit.

"Get rid of it. I don't care."

I gave away a dresser and the dining room chairs. We bought a new fridge and stocked it with food she liked. We picked up dozens of pink and white roses, and they stood around the apartment like guests trying too hard to please.

Nelly wiped the table and told me my mother wasn't going to like the fact that the kitchen didn't have a window. I nodded in agreement, but what could I do? She had picked the place.

My mother pointed out that the master bathroom didn't have a tub. She loved a good long bath. Was that too much to ask?

After a week of going back and forth from home to her apartment, after hiring her several part-time aides—she disliked all of them—I began to ask myself why had I let her move here, without a kitchen window or a tub? What was I thinking?

She said to me one night, "I can't possibly live here. I'm going to move out." She folded up the napkin near her coffee cup. "I'll go back to the Sutton. I don't like Connecticut."

The next morning, she took the one suitcase Nelly had packed for her, ordered a car, and moved back into the Sutton.

That evening, I got a call.

"It's gone down since I was last here."

"You were only there last month."

"Yes, but they're not as attentive. They must be under new management."

In the meantime, I had begged the super and landlord to allow us to break the lease. No doubt because my mother had complained so often, the super was willing to help; he knew someone who would sublet the apartment. She also, I soon discovered, told her lawyer to write a letter claiming she had to move into an assisted living home, due to her poor health.

165

The movers hauled everything into storage. My mother paid for all the moves, but they totaled up to one tremendous waste. Whatever happened to the point, that one she had made so adamantly weeks ago, that she was worried about money?

A few days later, I picked my mother up from the hotel so she could spend the week with me. I told her I'd looked at a small apartment in an assisted living home called The Greens, which was new, tastefully decorated, and close to me.

I took her to see it, and she said, "This is Connecticut, isn't it?"

My sister came to visit us over the weekend. My mother told her she didn't want to move into the assisted living apartment. "It doesn't seem like the right place, does it?" she asked my sister, hoping she'd be her ally.

But my sister toughened. "If you don't at least try this new situation, we're not going to have anything to do with you."

My mother glared at her sideways. "Fine, force me into a nursing home."

We both softened. We told her it wasn't a nursing home. We told her she'd have help and physical therapy. The apartment was manageable, cozy. We told her how nice Connecticut could be.

She started out in a studio, as there were no one-bedrooms available at the time. None of the apartments, I discovered, had a tub. There was, instead, a shower with a metal bar for safety.

I heard from her within a day, "The food is horrible. I haven't eaten a thing since I arrived, and you realize, Lori, I can't take my bath."

I said, "Why don't we go out for dinner?"

After dinner, back at her studio, she told the boys to go downstairs with Doug and ask for cookies. When Alex and Ben hesitated, she called the kitchen as if she were ringing room service: "I've got some hungry little boys here. Can you send up a plate of those delicious chocolate chip cookies?"

The kitchen staff complied.

Then my mother instructed the boys to fetch a ball from the car, so they could play catch in the hall. "Go liven up the place. It's so dead here."

They were too shy, and she walked into the hall and got them going. "That's right. Good catch. Faster now."

After a few months, she moved into a one-bedroom, and when I went to see it, she said, "I don't socialize with the residents here for the simple reason that they're all so terribly dull. They take art classes. Fat chance you're going to get me to decorate some clay pot with a fucking tulip in it."

She preferred to socialize with the director, who was in her forties. She ordered pizza and asked the director to join her.

In time, I took my mother to see another assisted living place in New York, but she liked it even less than where she was, and, in the car, I heard about how the nurses woke her too early and waited for her to take her pills. I'd been told that they were wary of her self-medicating, as they'd found pills on the floor. She reported the nurses to the director.

The director recommended that the visiting psychiatrist speak to my mother once a week. "After all, this isn't what she's used to," the director said, "It's not home." Hearing those words from someone I didn't know at all disturbed me.

After she met with the psychiatrist, my mother called. "Yes, Dr. Roberts came to talk to me. She's no rocket scientist. I was analyzing her after ten minutes."

After 9/11, Nelly decided to return to Baltimore, where her husband lived.

My mother said to me, "Now that Nelly is no longer with you, maybe I can live with you. I'll pay you rent."

I felt crushed by her request. I couldn't bear the thought of my mother haunting my day with her dissatisfactions. I thought of my children and the streaks of meanness they would face, and I told my mother that she'd be miserable in our house.

"We're so disorganized; we'd drive you crazy," I said.

She didn't bring it up again, and she slowly began to transform, as if the idea of living in a place designed to assist her had also inspired her to become a woman with a multitude of new needs. The boys offered her, here and there, a glimpse at joy, but, after a while, even their laughter couldn't break through to her.

She rarely got dressed in the morning, and she slept much of the day.

On occasion, I invited her to spend the weekend. I tried to enliven her. I cooked her favorite meals; we watched movies. There were moments when I looked at her, particularly when she didn't know it, and I felt so much for her that love rushed into my head unexpectedly and I had to breathe in and allow the feeling.

Our guest bedroom had its own bathroom. There was a shower, no tub. I just wanted her to relax in a tub. If she could take a bath—and she hadn't in far too long—she would be happy for the moment. I was convinced: she would lose herself in the warmth of the scented water. I suggested that she use our tub upstairs, and Doug and I held her arms as she managed each step. At the top, she looked around.

"Never been up here. How many bedrooms do you have?" She glanced up and down the hall, suspicious, no doubt thinking I had plenty of room for her.

In my bathroom, she studied the tub. "I'll never be able to get in. It's too deep."

Suddenly it did seem like a bottomless tub. I continued to run the water anyway and helped her in. Getting her out was even harder.

My mother never went back upstairs.

She never took another bath.

The next time she visited, I helped her shower. Afterwards, she waddled into the guest bedroom, where she swallowed her tranquilizer, her blood thinner, her anti-vertigo pill, and then she slipped into bed. She padded her body with several pillows.

It was eight o'clock.

"Good night, Mom."

I called the kids in. They rushed over to her and gave her a kiss.

"Good night, everyone," she said. "Leave a light on out there, just in case."

I turned one on in the bathroom, and, just in case, another in the hall.

Sunday in May

The rain was steady, and I wondered if my mother would cancel our dinner plans. She didn't like to go out in the rain, but it was Mother's Day, and she wanted to celebrate. We decided to eat on the early side, hoping to beat the dinner crowds. The nearby restaurants my mother liked, the ones that weren't too expensive and also appropriate for young boys, didn't take reservations.

By the time we arrived at The Greens, the rain was a satin sheet. My mother had managed to get downstairs by herself (I usually went up to fetch her) and was standing behind her walker, with her cane lying across the top, like a cross warding off evil spirits. I took her cane, helped her into the car, and folded the walker into the trunk.

She asked the boys if they were hungry. She was trying to be cheerful. Doug drove slowly on the wet streets and pulled up to the sidewalk of the Chinese restaurant to drop us off.

"I'll just take the cane. Leave the walker," my mother said.

We scuttled inside the small entrance, the boys ahead of me, my mother beside me, and could hardly fit in the vestibule, where a horde of people was already waiting for tables.

"We'll be here forever," my mother announced, immediately irritated. "Didn't you make a reservation?"

"They don't take them," I said. "It moves fast."

Her eyes closed and she looked away. She shuffled from side to side and then shot me a dirty look. "I'd sit on my walker if I had it," she said. "But there's no room in here anyway."

A woman in her forties, who was standing with her husband and young daughter, glanced up to Doug, who had just come in from parking the car, and asked, "Excuse me, aren't you that Disney actor?"

He chuckled. "No, I wish I were."

"Well, you look just like him. I can't remember his name. You probably wouldn't tell me even if you were," she said, blushing.

"Go ahead. You're the VIP. Ask for a table," my mother said to Doug, momentarily lightening up.

At that moment three or four more people swarmed in. A table near the door became available, and the waitress began frantically wiping it clean, when my mother said to the hostess, "Can we have that table?

"No, I'm sorry. There are a few people before you."

When no one claimed the table within the next minute or two, my mother did.

"Mom," I said, hurrying over to her. "What are you doing? There are people ahead of us."

"Oh, stop trying to please everyone. No one's sitting here. If we just sit down they're not going to ask us to leave. You're such a goodie-good. Just sit down, Lori."

The hostess trotted over, followed by the family whose table my mother had taken.

I said, "Come on, Mom, I'll get you a chair."

"I don't want a fucking chair. It figures I'd have to wait around when I'm in so much pain. What do you care, Lori? Why can't I sit here?" she asked the hostess. "I'm not well. What's the difference?"

"Madam, these people are waiting, too. They were here first."

"Can you please give her a chair to sit on? I'm sorry, but she can't stand for long," I told the hostess. She quickly brought over a chair, and my mother took her time sitting down.

"Another great Mother's Day," she said. "Thanks a lot."

And I walked away, heading outside, trying to remain under the canopy of the shopping strip, but the rain was slapping at my side. I drifted down to the end of the strip, away from the crowds, and started crying. I didn't want the boys to see me. I was always trying to hide how she made me feel. I was always explaining away her bitterness. Whenever the boys complained about seeing her, both Doug and I would say, "Sometimes you have to do things you may not want to do for others. To make them happy."

But there they were, my twins, blond hair flying as they raced over to me, relieved to be able to run, also eager to get away. I'd been caught.

"Mommy, are you okay?"

I was still crying; in their presence the tears spilled faster. "I'm sorry. It's just very hard to please her. She can be so tough, but she's in pain. I'll be fine. I'm sorry."

Alex touched my back, Ben my arm. He said, "It's okay. Let's go back inside. Let's eat."   Alex hugged me, and I was no longer crying. I took their hands and went back to my mother.

Within a few minutes we were given a table. My mother hooked her cane on the back of the chair and commented on the smallness of the table. She took out her reading glasses. I told myself to forget my anger. Doug tended to the boys in a doting, comical manner, his way of riding through her unkindness.

"Don't put the glass so close to the edge," he said. "When you were really little, you'd tip the glass when it was full. That was fun, remember?" He smiled as if they were so much older.

"Well, here we are, another Mother's Day," I said.

"What'd you get her, Doug?"

Doug rarely gave me a Mother's Day gift. We'd go out for dinner, but gifts were not something he was a big believer in, particularly for a day (and Father's Day qualified, too) he viewed as outright foolish. My mother knew this, of course.

"Well," he said, "she has the boys here, and me, and we try to be pretty good to her."

"Let's order," I said.

"Oh, yes, I know, Douglas," my mother told him, smirking. "You give her your undying love. That's what her father always used to say, too."

"Ah," I said and exhaled, placing my napkin on my lap. The waitress came over. Not bothering to ask my mother what she'd like to drink, I quickly ordered, "I'll have a Chardonnay, if you have it, please."

A Show of Affection

In February of 2004, our family decided to drive down to Florida for winter break and stay with my mother-in-law in Boca Raton. We drove so we could bring our dog, Sophie, a large Shepherd mix, who'd become too difficult in her old age to leave alone or in a kennel. As always, I'd left my itinerary with the nurses at The Greens.

After a few days in Boca Raton, the head nurse called me. "We're sending your mother to Norwalk hospital. She won't eat."

We returned to New York. My mother was in a room on the telemetry floor. The admitting doctor had noted a mild heart attack. She still hadn't eaten, and more tests were being ordered. In the meantime, she hadn't been given her Valium, which she had been subsisting on for the past thirty years, and her body was protesting.

My mother lay in bed, steaming in anger. She was wearing a flimsy blue hospital gown. Her hair was straight and short, tucked behind her ears. It hadn't turned gray. Her face looked smooth, soothed by her nightly treatments of moisturizer. But the rest of her body was suffering. She had gained even more weight, and her feet were deformed from bunions and a past surgery that had been a disaster, causing her right big toe to splay out. After having experienced more than one painful dental procedure, she had surrendered to dentures, the last straw for her. I turned away and blamed myself for failing to improve her life.

She was almost eighty.

"You better get me the fuck out of here; they're going to kill me. I will die here, I will, and my death will hang over your head."

I sighed, reassured her she'd live, and backed out of the room to page the doctor.

"You have to give her something to relax," I said.

"We'll give her Ativan. It's better than Valium."

"Okay," I said, relieved, but some time later, I thought, she's eighty years old. Why try to get her off something she has relied on for years?

The next afternoon I approached her with news the doctor had just given me. The Ativan had calmed her a little.

"Your gall bladder's really infected. They have to remove it. That's why you have no appetite and why you feel so bad."

"I always feel bad."

"I mean the way you're feeling now."

"And you know how I'm feeling, I suppose. I don't give a shit about these doctors and their opinions. I don't trust any of them, and the nurse, the nurse hits me at night."

"What are you talking about? Which nurse?"

"The one last night."

I told her I'd look into that right away but then asked her again about the surgery, which would be laparoscopic, and much less invasive.

"Oh, I don't care. I'm going to die anyway."

It was going to be a long haul with her, surgery, recovery, rehab, without one nod of gratitude in my direction. I told myself I didn't need gratitude.

"Look at the bruises on my arms," she said, without missing another beat.

Her arm was bruised.

I asked the floor receptionist about the nurse and my mother's bruises. Perhaps the nurse had just not been gentle enough, I said to the woman behind the desk. My mother was fragile; my mother was nervous. Later, another nurse explained to me that my mother's skin was thin, and the slightest pressure, say the elastic band they used to take blood, could make bruises bloom.

I went home, exhausted, to my husband, my sons, and my dog, who was also quite sick at the time, but, at least, she was eating. She was affectionate and felt warm, and I stretched out next to her.

In bed that night, I reviewed all that I had to take care of the next day for my mother. My sister was living in California, in daily contact with me, and I conferred with her. I thought about the past fifteen years; there had always been something wrong with my mother: her teeth, her ears, her back, her feet. It seemed impossible to tell just how serious anything really was, and with every new doctor and every new treatment, her problems became more unbearable, and she'd threaten a doctor with a malpractice suit.

I held my mother's hand in the recovery room after the surgery. She was the only one in the room. A nurse stood down the hall, busy with paperwork. The tubes, the peculiar breaths working their way through my mother's body, alarmed me, but she looked peaceful. The surgeon had failed to remove the gall bladder laparoscopically. The organ, already too diseased, had attached itself to the pancreas; the surgeon had been forced to cut my mother open. At her age, the recovery, I was warned, would be slow.

After a few days, she found she couldn't walk. The doctors had no explanation. She may be giving up, they told me. She had experienced that mild heart attack the day she'd been admitted, but to repair her valves, even test her heart at her age... They would need her permission.

When I went to talk to her, she was still, blinking at the ceiling. "Don't leave me here—I'm scared to be here."

"You're really sick. You can't go home now."

"I don't want any more operations. I'm an old woman. I've had enough. Just make me comfortable."

"You could try physical therapy, try to get stronger, no matter what the doctors say. The fact that the arteries in your neck are almost clogged is nothing new. We've known that for years." Two decades earlier, a neurologist had informed my mother of the dangers of a blocked artery, but her heart had been just fine until now.

Later, I reviewed the facts with the doctor. I looked down the hall, while the doctor advised me on the next step. The walls needed new paint. The tiles were stained. Deterioration circled me; it was what I chose to notice.

Should I offer her a reprieve from this place? I considered bringing my mother home to live with me, yet I still felt protective of my family.

I took my mother back to the assisted living home and hired full-time nurses. Her apartment wasn't yet set up for someone in a wheelchair, and after one day I got a call that she was back in the hospital, complaining of chest pain.

My sister flew to New York. We visited my mother every day. She was irritable, depressed, and weary.

"Mommy, why don't I get you a sandwich from the deli across the street?" my sister asked. She had a perky voice that was almost maternal when addressing my mother.

"That sounds good."

The sandwich came; my mother ate very little.

"It tastes strange," she said. "Everything tastes bad to me."

My sister left at the end of the week. She had to get back to her family.

There was my mother's living will: do not resuscitate, no feeding tubes, keep her comfortable. I had to plan. I took a few days to check out several nursing homes. That was a world of sadness in itself, and it forced me, for the moment, to step out of mine. The nicer ones—and one or two were quite luxurious—had waiting lists, including the one affiliated with The Greens.

There was another in New Canaan that could admit her on a temporary rehabilitative basis. I called my sister and told her I liked the facility; it was close by, clean, attractive, and small. Abstract bronze sculptures, made by a resident, decorated the lobby.

Once admitted, my mother, to my surprise, began physical therapy. She thought, no doubt, that if she regained some of her strength she could leave. Then came the different psychiatric medications—anti-anxiety, anti-psychotic, whatever potion would make her adapt—given to her by psychiatrists I'd never met but

176

spoke to on the phone. One medication made her act as if she had undergone a lobotomy. Angry, I told the doctors to take her off it and to stop prescribing new pills.

I wanted my mother, not a silent replica.

"Would you like to go back to The Greens?"

A staff psychologist, a woman in her thirties, was asking my mother questions to determine her state of mind.

My mother sat in a wheelchair, in a common area, wearing a pressed white blouse and navy pants.

"The Greens? Oh, yes, that would be nice."

"So you liked it there?"

"Well, you know, it's clean. And the nurses, the aides are all quite nice to me. It's a bit homey, and I know where everything is."

I could see how frightened she was. She joined her hands in her lap and held her head up high. What if the wrong answer slipped out? She didn't want to remain at the nursing home. She wanted to please so they'd say she could leave.

I wanted to hold her.

"Do you think you'd like to continue with physical therapy?" the psychologist asked.

"Oh, yes, I did rather well today. You know, a bit of leg lifts, and I even took a step or two with help from the therapist."

"Very well, Mrs. Toppel, then we'll schedule you for a session tomorrow. Have a nice night. Shall I have your dinner sent over here so you can eat with your daughter?"

"That would be very kind of you, dear." She then turned to me. "Ducks, you'll get me a few new blouses. You know, so I don't have to iron anything. I have no iron."

Ducks was a childhood nickname that belonged to my cousin, although my mother, sometimes, liked to lend it to me. As for the iron, my mother never ironed; others had always done that for her.

I said, "Okay, I'll do that tomorrow. I'll pick you up three or four shirts."

"Mostly white ones. White looks fresh."

When her dinner came, a tray of stew, pudding, and juice, she ate one or two bites just to satisfy me.

The next morning, I was about to leave for Lord & Taylor's to shop for her blouses when the nursing home called.

My mother was refusing breakfast and wouldn't get dressed.

At first, she occupied the room by herself, although it was a double, but within a few days a woman, who had fallen and broken her hip, moved in. My mother liked her privacy, so I started taking her to the garden in a wheelchair. We talked in the shade.

"I saw Eileen yesterday," my mother said.

"Oh?" Her sister had been dead for over thirty years.

"I got off the train, and she was there to meet me. She looks very good; she was wearing a nice suit. She always looks good though, doesn't she, Lollipop?"

There, that was the right nickname. From then on, my mother began using endearing words, and to my shock, she never stopped. Her meanness and disappointment had been killed with whatever else was eating away at her insides. As her strength receded, her memory was taking center stage. She was happy again, eager to share good news, and her eyes beamed as she told me stories. Her smile reminded me of when I was a child, as did her laugh, which made her chin tuck into her neck.

"Yes, Aunt Eileen is beautiful," I said.

"Always was, was my father's favorite, you know."

"I know. What else did you two do?"

"Oh, she had to leave. We're going to meet up again tomorrow. With Peter, Peter's coming, too."

Peter, her younger brother, dead for more than ten years.

Sometime that week, Sophie stopped eating her food. We began giving her people food, whatever she'd take.

"Sophie's barely eating. I think she's just so tired," I told my mother. She was fond of our dog, even though, generally, she was petrified of big dogs. It was just like her to be fond of Sophie, whom everyone else feared.

"I know how she feels," she said.

One morning, my husband and I found my mother in her room, lying in bed, caught in the fit of a high fever. Her skin was pink, her muscles twitching.

"Come here," she said to me, "I love you. I'm so sorry for anything I've ever done to hurt you. You've been a great daughter. And I love you, I love you, I love you, I love you."

I said to the nurse, "There's something wrong. She's saying good-bye. You have to take her to the hospital."

"We're waiting for the doctor."

"Call an ambulance," I said.

Doug was silent for a few seconds, rubbing his chin. He turned to the nurse. "This is obviously a different state she's in. I don't know what you're waiting for."

The ambulance was called. I rode in it with my mother. At the hospital she was given medication to reduce the fever. It was late, and Doug and I went home.

As soon as I woke up, I went to see her. The fever hadn't gone completely away.

"I won," she said to me.

She was in a new room, where the sunlight was a presence.

"You won what?" I tried to smile.

"I won the swimming race. My father's very proud. I'm a very good swimmer. I came in first. I won."

"I'm so proud of you," I said and hugged her.

"Isn't that great, Lol? I won."

"You won."

My mother returned to the nursing home in New Canaan. After consulting with all layers of the medical staff, we put her in hospice care. The decision was prompted by an infection that began sweeping through her body; the high fever wouldn't leave. She was given a room with a view of a fountain that stood in the same garden I'd taken her to earlier that week, but her bed wasn't close to the window. She shared the room with another woman on hospice, who had been living in the nursing home for a year or so.

"Does she like it here?" I asked the woman's daughter, who was there about as much as I was.

"I think so. But she's taking Oxycontin. She's been a little out of it."

"What's wrong with her?"

"She's had bad liver problems. They have her on morphine, which I could use right about now."

Her mother died a few days later. The family kept the body in the room, the curtains shut, so everyone could say good-bye. I tried to peek through a slit in the curtain, but I couldn't even view the bed. Although I was forty-four, I'd never seen a dead body. My disrespect for the family's loss didn't surprise me. I was only thinking of my own impending loss and how it might all look when laid out in a room.

My mother wouldn't take the antibiotics she needed to fight the infection. She wouldn't allow them to administer the medicine through an IV. The nurses pointed out that she wasn't eating anyway. She drank water, and water helped her last.

My mother was barely talking. She listened, she looked, sometimes she nodded, and she held my hand. For a woman who had spent so many years acting as if she should be treated like royalty, she had mastered a majestic look even in her weakness—she appeared aloof and watchful. In a way, she looked beautiful, and even the rabbi, whom I had asked to come to say a prayer for her—that seemed important at the time—commented on how youthful her face was.

"Mom, do you want me to stay with you tonight?"

A squeeze of the hand. A nod.

I pulled up a chair, opened up a book I'd brought from home: Kipling's collection of poetry. I began to read from her favorite poem, "If."

I called my sister and she flew back to New York. Together, we were determined to make my mother eat and offered her juice and milkshakes through a straw. We crushed the antibiotic in the milkshake.

Once, I refilled the milkshake before my mother had finished the first cup.

My sister yelled, "What are you doing? Now we won't know how much medicine she took. What's wrong with you?"

She left to take a walk. It was early April. The trees were filling, and some azalea bushes had reddened. My sister and I apologized to each other after she returned to the room. We sat by the bed, and every four to six hours, a nurse came padding into the room to squeeze a syringe full of morphine under my mother's tongue.

"Tell her it's okay to let go," the social worker told us.

The day after my sister left for California, a nurse called me before six a.m. to tell me my mother didn't have long; her breathing had changed. Within a half hour, I was at her side. Doug stayed home to put the boys on the school bus.

I was alone with her when she died, and I rushed out of the room and down the hall to the nurses' front desk. I passed several residents whose minds were either destroyed or at rest and whose bodies still wrestled within their square foot of the world. Their presence had always felt profound, yet suddenly I had no idea they were even there.

"I think she's gone," I said to the nurse. "My mother."

"My God," the nurse whispered and jumped up. She trotted ahead of me down the hall, but I passed her and saw that she was crying.

Doug arrived. Before my mother had become so sick, he had

stored up little patience for her. She had insulted him, accused him, and criticized him. But in this past month, for me, he had sat beside her, talked to her, and soothed her. He had made friends with the nurses and aides, and that friendliness, whenever he visited, felt like gentle music.

Now he said, shaking his head, "She just had to pick our anniversary."

It was April 11, our wedding anniversary.

I called Daphne, a close friend, who drove right over. While Doug spoke to the nurses about the next step, Daphne and I walked outside to my car. Even though the day was clear and cool, the most likable kind of spring day, we sat in the car. Daphne is tall and blond; I'm short and dark. We sat side by side, she understanding my grief (her own mother was sick), and my taking in her willingness to be there. We sat side by side, and I felt that we must look alike. A mother's death can do that, if only for a few seconds.

She had brought hot coffee, and I sipped mine, grateful to have it. I can't remember all we talked about, but whatever was said, I do remember, mattered.

I made several decisions alone. Doug and my sister offered to help, but, for the most part, I chose to be on my own. I picked out a rose-colored headstone (my mother hated grey), a pine coffin, and a linen shroud (my mother had made me promise not to spend a lot of money at her funeral; after all, no one would know). Both choices followed one of the oldest Jewish traditions of burial, simple encasements, so one's body returned to the earth quickly. I was relieved with the idea of the shroud. A shroud was imperious. In the end, my mother hadn't really liked any of her clothes anyway.

My sister and I talked over what to put on her headstone. Finally, from *The Wizard of Oz*, those words my mother loved so much, a refrain from our childhood:

182

Somewhere over the rainbow skies are blue
And the dreams that you dare to dream really do come true…

April vanished. Sophie was eating less and less. By October, she was clearly suffering, and we put her to sleep. I adopted two puppies. They took up much of my spare time, and the summer passed, the new year came, and soon winter and spring.

One evening in June, I was sitting with my sons, both twelve, in the den. Alex was beside me on the couch, and Ben sat in a chair, eating ice cream. We were watching a reality show, one that we all found entertaining. The dogs were lying on the couch, asleep, while Doug was in our bedroom, watching a baseball game.

I said, "I miss my mother. I know she was tough to be around, and that's what you remember. But I remember her when I was younger."

Ben glanced at me; he wasn't sure how to respond.

"It's just that she wasn't always difficult," I said.

"She used to give us money whenever she saw us. She gave us a lot," Ben said and then dug his spoon into the ice cream.

He was offering up one of his few fond memories, which isn't to say that giving money every time a grandmother sees her grandson was my idea of an admirable show of affection, but for my mother that kind of generosity—its ease and honesty—was a constant.

"She loved you, and that's how she showed it," I said.

"Sometimes she was in a good mood," Alex added, taking his eyes off the television to meet mine. I smiled as he twirled a strand of his hair around his forefinger, his signal for sleepiness.

I said, "I thought you should know I miss her."

It was getting late, and I turned off the television. The boys started up the stairs first, then I followed, and the dogs trotted past me.

We all settled into our own beds, while the night carried on.

Susan

Susan with her mother, Selma Wenesky Rubin

Slipping Out from Under

My left thumb is identical to my right thumb except for a small pink callus below its joint, permanently hardened by the regular pressure of my lower teeth. I am in my fifties—writer, teacher, wife, and mother of two grown daughters—and I still suck my thumb. The left one, never the right; an ingrained response, I know, from my earliest days.

When my first baby was born, my mother revealed that she had to stop nursing me after just three weeks because of an infection in her left nipple. My parents had come to stay in our Brooklyn Heights apartment to meet their new granddaughter. My mother and I were sitting on opposite corners of the sofa when she told me. Sofie lay across my lap and pulled greedily at my right breast; my mother perched upright on the edge of the seat cushion, knees together.

I remember her words, innocent, almost chatty, her eyes averted across the living room as she spoke. Of course I have no memory of my own first weeks, but I can imagine: the very best thing in my new life—my sustenance, my comfort, my reconnection with my mother's body—suddenly gone. The discovery of my thumb set a lasting pattern: get the need filled, find another way. Though I don't think about it often, I know my left thumb holds something of my mother for me.

In my childhood memories of her, she is often standing on the sidelines as my father proclaimed, announced, questioned, yelled. She is silent and passive, removed. In the memoir class, after I'd finish reading my work, Joan's response was often the same: "But what about your mother? Where was she?"

The fall that our writing group started meeting, my father was declining into the morass of Alzheimer's disease. Over five years our family had watched him slowly disappear. I talked to my mother on the telephone almost every day, and traveled regularly to Washington, D.C., to visit. Sometimes she cried, from exhaustion or despair.

But the more lost my father became, the more my mother emerged. As I wrote about her and shared my stories in our group, and as I learned about the others' mothers through the stories they wrote, my understanding started to shift. For the first time in my life, I began to glimpse who my mother was.

I am the only member of our writing group whose mother is still alive, who can still ask her mother questions, compare memories from the past. When I think of the others' stories—the heartbreaking last days of Vicki and Lori's mothers, the spreading of Joan's mother's ashes—I sense the fragility of the time I have left with my own mother. I have just begun to discover her. It awakens a hunger I can hardly bear to feel.

I Love You Still

"*It had to be you, it had to be you…*" I hear my mother singing and look up from my book to see her cutting vegetables in the kitchen. I've driven from New York without my husband, Paul, to visit her in her suburban home outside of Washington for a few days.

It has been less than six months since my father died, and my mother, at eighty-two, is determined to stay in this house where she has been living alone since he entered a nursing home two years earlier, and where they had lived together since 1971, the year I started college.

I recognize the tune; it is one I've heard her sing before. My mother has always sung aloud, her voice accompanying the radio or ringing out above the congregation in the synagogue. She sang sweetly, harmonizing with my father, "*Inchworm, inchworm, measuring the marigolds.*" As a teenager, she won a talent contest with her rendition of "Melancholy Baby" and performed it on the radio.

She stops and turns toward me. Her hair is mostly gray now, cut very short around her head, and her skin is soft in the powdery way that skin can age. "I've always liked that song," she says, "but only recently did I realize how appropriate the words are for me and Dad." I try to recall the lyrics, but all I can think is, *It had to be you.*

She turns back to her chopping, and goes on to recite some of the lines. "*Somebody who could make me be true, could make me be blue,*" and then, "*Some others I've seen, might never be mean, but they wouldn't do…*"

Blue? Mean? What is she saying?

"*With all your faults I love you still,*" my mother sings.

My mother is standing by the dining table where my father, my brothers, and I are seated; she is rigid behind the chair from which she has just risen. I am in my early teens. We are mid-meal, food on our yellow and white dishes, silverware poised in our hands. My mother has accidentally knocked over a glass of milk. The noise of its clinking against a serving bowl has halted all other sound, and the air in the room has frozen. The only movement is the slow spread of milk as it travels along the surface of the table and over its edge. I focus on the smooth whiteness.

"What were you thinking?" my father says. His voice is harsh, strained. I keep my head down, my gaze now fixed on my half-eaten tuna salad. There are blueberries in the pattern on the plate. "Why don't you look before you do things?" He is reaching out to interrupt the milk with his napkin. Disturbance surrounds him.

My mother hasn't moved. When I look up at her, I see her eyes are pink and shiny. She turns her head to the side, then walks into the kitchen. I am pressed flat, too young to identify the pain I feel for her. My father shakes his head. No one speaks.

I always believed my father loved my mother. He told me things like, "My life didn't start till I met your mother," and, "Your mother, she's an *eshet chayall*—a woman of valor." When he said those things, his eyes were filled with pride. He helped her clear the table and clean the kitchen after meals. When they made salad, she peeled the carrots and he diced them. One day my mother confided to me that she wished she could make a salad on her own once in a while.

"Baruch atah, adonai…" My mother's voice is a clear stream flowing beside my father's tenor, as my brothers and I mumble beneath them. It is Friday night, and we are lighting the Sabbath candles as the sun goes down. We gather in the kitchen like this every week; we are expected to be home. My mother unties her apron, takes it from her waist, and folds it into quarters before putting it in a drawer.

My parents each brought Judaism with them to their marriage, and turned to its rituals to give structure to our family. They deepened their observance together over time.

Two brass candlesticks placed on a metal tray hold the stocky white candles that my mother has lit. She blows gently to extinguish the match, then places it on the tray before raising her hands and holding them, palms down, toward the flame. She closes her eyes and begins to sing the blessing. We all join in, my father's voice boisterous. I cannot stop staring at her.

Her expression is serious, her brow slightly furrowed, the line where her lids meet betraying the smallest amount of pressure. An arc of candlelight illuminates the lower half of her face. There is faded red lipstick on her lips. Her hands do not move.

When the prayer is over, she stands still, quiet for what to me seems an uncomfortably long time. The murmur of water boiling on the stove plays with the sizzle of roasting chicken, and I am hungry. I try to imagine what she is saying to God, which one of us she is most worried about, but I can never be sure. Then, with a tiny nod, her eyes open and her hands drop. "Good *Shabbos*, good *Shabbos*, good *Shabbos*," we say, as we each peck the other on the cheek.

My father's presence defined the nature of our family and the mood in our home. He could be jovial, spewing jokes, telling stories. He taught us, helped us with our schoolwork. We were captive to his words.

But he also had a near-obsessive need for control, and an unpredictable temper. Crumbs on the countertop, hairs in the sink, lights left on in empty rooms provoked his anger. Waste was despicable, carelessness scorned. He spit curses under his breath. We all—including my mother—treaded lightly, remaining on guard against a sudden shift that could trigger his rage.

It hurts me to say that my mother cowered before my father. Terrified of setting him off, and forbearing perhaps to a fault, she rarely confronted or disagreed with him. When he directed his ire at me, which he did with increasing frequency as I moved through adolescence, she was mute. I never saw them hug each other. In my memories, she rarely speaks, never laughs.

I watch as my mother flings a white tablecloth over the bridge table she has unfolded beside the fireplace in our living room. The fabric floats into place; she tugs at a corner and flattens the cloth with her hands. I am wearing pajamas, elastic-waist pants with a long-sleeved shirt that buttons. It is New Year's Eve, and my mother is setting a special table where she and my father will eat dinner after my brothers and I are asleep. There are fluted glasses and candlesticks. I am seven.

They celebrate this way every year, though I have never been awake to see them. In my imagination, they face each other, candlelight between them. My mother wears a dress, dark blue trimmed in white; her lips are red and her cheeks are rouged. They start with grapefruit halves, each topped with a maraschino cherry, and then have baked potato and steak that they cut with wooden-handled knives. Music plays quietly on the record player.

As it nears midnight, my father opens a bottle of Champagne that my mother has brought from the kitchen. He pours half-glasses that they clink. "Happy New Year," they say. "*L'chaim.*" Together, they carry their plates back to the kitchen and clean up everything except the bridge table, which I will find bare in the morning. They don't usually stay up this late, so as soon as they've finished, they head up to sleep.

My mother is reaching toward my father with a Kleenex, attempting to wipe his nose. He jerks his head away, his face contorting. "Get the fuck away from me," he shouts, and glares at her with disgust.

My mother withdraws, an awkward smile emerging. "I was just..." she begins.

"Shut up! Shut up!" My father's voice is rough and growly, then he lowers his head and is quiet.

I have come to Washington to help my mother take care of my

father, who has sunk into the Alzheimer's he was diagnosed with shortly after being hit by a car several years earlier. He is eighty-two, confined now to a wheelchair because of a variety of physical problems. Sometimes he radiates sweetness and love, but other times, erratically, he lashes out in anger and insult. He knows who we are but he doesn't absorb much of what goes on around him. When you talk to him, it's hard to gauge whether he understands what you're saying. His greatest pleasure comes from eating.

My mother has retired from her position as a librarian, a profession she took on after my brothers and I were grown. She completed her master's degree the same year I graduated from high school, and continued working even after my father stopped. From the day he was hit by the car, though, her life has revolved around his care. I have visited regularly enough to know her routine. I am there beside her during my stays, but it is she who remains with him hour after hour when I go, updating me on his progress on the phone each evening.

For days she sat in his hospital room as he lay in a coma. For weeks after he awoke she called for nurses to change his diapers and bring him juice. She read aloud to him from Homer's *Odyssey* and *Time* magazine, and took up her knitting when he fell asleep. When he was well enough to begin rehabilitation, she learned the exercises he was to do and helped him move his arms and legs, lift, down, lift, down, until he insisted she stop. Finally he was able to come home, where she had a motorized lift installed to bring him up and down the stairs, and where aides came and sat on the sofa in the den when they had no work to do.

At night, my father called out her name. "Selma! Selllmmaa!" She adjusted his head, shifted his leg. He woke often, and sometimes his exhales were extended groans repeated with each breath. My mother barely slept. Soon she had an aide come for the night, and she took to sleeping in one of the upstairs bedrooms with the door closed.

On this day, she is in the kitchen making lunch. I sit with my father in the dining room, his wheelchair pushed up to the table beside me. He is silent, staring vacantly in front of him. The light is dim; raindrops scatter on the skylight above.

My mother serves us plates already arranged with food: slices of leftover chicken, vegetables mixed into a salad, a pile of cut corn. My father will eat whatever he is given; she apportions his servings so he will not gain weight. "He's already hard enough to move," she tells me.

Sometimes my father shines with his love for my mother. He stares at her, his eyes glued to her every move like a baby's. His face is soft, a slight smile on his lips.

But now he is sour. He shovels the corn into his mouth.

"Do you want a glass of juice?" my mother asks him, gently leaning in toward his cheek.

"Do you want a glass of juice?" He mimics her, the words singsong, his face scornful. It's part of the Alzheimer's, we've been told, but we recognize my father's rage, now unshackled.

"Fucking bitch!" he barks.

My mother turns abruptly and walks out of the room. "Don't speak to her like that," I tell him, but he doesn't look at me. A few minutes pass before she returns, the rims of her eyes red.

Today, my mother and I linger after breakfast. Sunshine from the skylight streams onto the newspapers, books, and magazines strewn around us. A radio broadcasts classical music. The house is still, empty, permeated with a calmness I never felt when my father was alive.

I skim the *Washington Post* as my mother works on a *New York Times* crossword puzzle from the previous Sunday, one that I finished before I came here. "Diamond center?" she says. "Diamond center?"

She is wearing a cardigan sweater she knitted for herself, a complicated pattern of overlapping stars in lavenders and blues, with silver buttons. Her pants are light brown corduroy and her shoes are beige, thick and round on feet that are planted flat on the floor. Her lips are pale, her shoulders faintly curved.

I get up and stand behind her, look down at the page. She smells like soap.

"Think baseball," I say. "It starts with M." After a pause, I tell her: "Mound."

She doesn't mind me giving her the answers. She fills in the letters with a pencil. She and my father used to finish the Sunday puzzle in an afternoon. Now she completes as many spaces as she can during the week.

When I am not there, we talk by telephone nearly every day. When she calls me, she might begin, "I just wanted to chat." When I call her, I ask her how she is, and she reports on the details of her day.

For exercise, she walks around the neighborhood as often as she can, takes a yoga class and tai chi for seniors. She works on her homework for the Hebrew language class she rejoined in the fall. She is in a book club, and she and her friend Zelda have tickets to a series of concerts. On Friday evenings, she lights the Sabbath candles; on Saturdays she goes to the synagogue. When the weather is good, she walks to a nearby movie theater and takes in a matinee. She cooks meals, fish or meat, roasted vegetables. She sets a place for herself at the table, lays out her pills beside the spoon. While she eats, she reads; she has cookies for dessert.

At night, she settles in the den to watch television. It is here that she ends her days. She sits in one of the two matching leather lounge chairs she and my father bought years before. She has an array of snacks she indulges in: crystallized ginger, chocolate covered almonds, frozen yogurt. She brings her selection from the kitchen in a small glass bowl and eats it slowly. Around eleven, she shuts out the lights and goes upstairs to bed.

Watching the Thunder

We are sitting downstairs in the living room, my mother, my brother Eric, and me. It is the house on Alpine Street in Arlington Heights, a middle-class suburb of Boston, the first house my parents owned. My brother David hasn't been born, so Eric must be only two and I just three. We have gathered here because of the storm, its thunderclaps exploding, each one louder and nearer than the one before, as if they're closing in on us. Lightning slices the room and I turn to my mother. My father has gone to Europe on business, leaving her to quell our fears.

It is after dinner, the grayness of summer rain clouds mingling with the approach of dusk. The windows are open so we can hear the panting of the wind and the static of the rainfall. The air is warm and smells like wetness. I burrow into the corner of an upholstered chair that is too large for me, and Eric sits beside my mother on the sofa across the room. The only movement is what I hear outside.

I am worried, and I study my mother for signs of reassurance. I think she is pretty with her dark brown hair curling along her cheeks and her skin paler than usual in the murky glow of the storm. Eric nestles against her arm, looking sleepy and comforted, but I am not sure I can trust my mother with my unease. It would have been my father who'd have taken charge had he been here; my mother, still and silent, her unfocused gaze landing on the carpet, seems to be offering nothing more than her presence as protection. But with each bolt of lightning and jolt of thunder, I realize I have no choice. I don't take my eyes from her, even as the light in the room dims with the night.

We'll stay like this until the thunder sounds like it's deep inside my ears and the lightning is easy to confuse with the blink of my heavy eyelids. Then we no longer hear the rain, and a calmness settles in. My mother stands. "Time for bed," she says, lifting Eric into her arms, and I follow her up the stairs.

Wasp

I am four years old and it is summertime, the sun making my eyes squint. My parents have invited friends for a barbecue, and everyone but my mother has gathered outside in the backyard. There are rows of bushes planted in straight lines that delineate the rear edges of the lawn. We're using the back doorway to get in and out of the house.

The doorway is at the top of a flight of stairs that leads to a wooden landing; there's a screen door and, inside, a heavy wooden door that today no one's bothering to close. I am up on the landing, about to enter the house, when I feel a tickle and look down. A fat brown wasp is perched on my inner left calf, between my stretched-out white sock and my scraped knee. Its body is slick and shiny against the paleness of my skin. Its wings quiver at its sides.

The moment I see it, I freeze, my right hand holding the screen door open. I've never been stung, but I've heard about wasps, how their bites are supposed to be the most painful. I am vaguely aware of the activity below me in the yard, the adults chatting at the plastic-covered table my parents have set up, the smoky smell of the hamburgers and hot dogs my father is flipping on the grill. My mother is inside, in the kitchen right around the corner.

I fix my eyes on the insect. "Mom!" I scream.

In an instant, she appears at the door, a red-and-white striped towel in her hand, a flowered apron tied around her waist. She leans toward me, her eyes serious with concern. For a moment she looks at my face, then spots the source of my terror. Without a word, she brushes the wasp off my leg with her towel. I watch it spiral upward toward the roof.

I am relieved, safe—until I look back at my mother's face. Her expression is stern; she is irritated. "You didn't have to scream so loud," she scolds. "And close the door—you're letting in the flies."

She has already disappeared inside as I let the door go and watch it bounce twice against its spring before it finally shuts.

Rearranging the Linen Closet

I sit cross-legged on the floor in the darkened upstairs hallway, five years old at most. It is nighttime and I am alone, my mother and father already asleep in their bedroom, Eric is in his crib in the room we share. The silence buzzes in my ears and makes me hear my breath.

I am peering into the linen closet, whose door, usually kept shut, I have opened. There is enough light creeping into the hall for me to see what I need. Not the stacks of sheets and towels on the upper shelves that tower above me: they are of no interest to me. It is the bottom of the closet that draws me, the floor-level drawer with a rounded slot that serves as a handle. I am there to rearrange things, lured from my bed by some pressing need.

I begin by sliding open the drawer, which is filled with bathroom supplies. There are rectangular boxes of tissues, rolls of toilet paper wrapped in crinkly paper. The toothpaste tubes are red and white, already slightly dented. The soap, Ivory, is packaged in blocks, each bar wrapped in blue and white paper. I love its pure white and the way it pops back up to the surface of the bathwater no matter how long you hold it down. The shampoo is Lustre Crème, in a white plastic tub with pink lettering. It is a thick, pearly-pink cream whose iridescence reminds me of jewelry.

I remove each item from its spot and place it on the floor beside me. It is a carpeted corridor, so I can work quietly until the drawer is empty and I am surrounded. Then one by one I put everything back, carefully positioning, lining up edges and fitting things in. Bigger items come first, straight lines stay together, uneven shapes are nudged into place to fill open spaces. I admire my work; by the time I am finished, the drawer looks snug and complete.

In my memory I sat there in the dark over and over again for months, though the image I carry is a single, unchanging impression. Was it really the middle of the night as it seemed, or

200

just after a little girl's bedtime? And why didn't my mother hear the springs in the mattress as I climbed in and out of bed, the padding of my feet in the hall, the jostling of bottles and boxes? I was never interrupted, and she never said a word.

My recollection ends before I've stood up, gone back to my room, and returned to bed. For many years, I imagined the child that I was then as sad and alone. When I became a mother, I told myself that I would not let one night pass with either of my daughters sitting by herself in a hallway, trying to impose order, take control, without me coming to her side to help.

Then a friend to whom I described my long-ago activity said she wished her own mother had given her such space to explore. "I'm sure she knew what you were doing," she told me, "but she let you be."

I want to believe that: that my mother was smarter than I ever knew, wise and deliberate.

School Shopping

My mother and I are the only shoppers in the girls' department, in a corner of the lower level of Filene's in Belmont Center. She sorts through the racks of sweaters and dresses. Her navy blue skirt falls just below her knees, her short-sleeved white blouse is tucked into her narrow waist, and she wears red flats on her stockinged feet. Over her right shoulder, a dark blue purse whose leather is quilted in a diamond pattern hangs by a gold chain.

"How about this?" she asks, holding up a maroon pleated skirt clipped to a wooden hanger. "It would go nicely with this." She reaches for a beige woolen pullover with patterning around the collar in the same shade of maroon. She places the sweater next to the skirt, outstretching her arms and leaning her head away from the clothing as if to see from a greater distance. "Look how the maroon in the sweater picks up the maroon in the skirt."

That was the day I learned the word maroon, a color that was everywhere in that section of the store. It was the summer of 1961, when I was seven and we moved to Belmont from nearby Arlington. My father had informed us repeatedly that in our new house my two younger brothers and I would have our own bedrooms. The only thing I recall about the move is that my parents let me choose the wallpaper for mine. From an oversized book of samples, I picked one that didn't seem old-fashioned: outlines of flowers floating between vertical red and pink stripes that looked like long, fat brushstrokes.

I spent much of my time that first summer in Belmont in my new bedroom. I rarely played with my brothers. Eric was a year and a half younger, and the few memories I have of him as a child involve either annoyance or disdain. He played more with David, who was only four. My parents were likely preoccupied with unpacking and setting up the house.

We gathered at the kitchen table for dinner. My father was the one who engaged us, who brought us picture books on Fridays when he got paid, and asked us questions as we ate. "Quick," he'd say, "who can remember what color socks you're wearing? Don't peek!" My brothers and I would look at each other until one of us took a stab, holding up a little leg as proof. When I think of my father during this period, he is untroubled, happy.

I see my mother from behind, straightening, dusting, folding clothes. I see her in front of the stove, stirring a large pot, flipping hamburgers in a frying pan. I see the ties of her apron, white with green stripes and bright red apples. Her head tilts forward and down, her short brown hair interrupting the soft line of her neck.

The Filene's in Belmont Center was a miniature version of the original store we'd visited often in downtown Boston. Our excursions there involved a bus that spewed and jolted its way to Cambridge and then an ever-crowded subway into the city. In the sprawling store, we used the escalators that drifted slowly upward, or sometimes the packed elevators that never missed a floor. My mother held my hand and walked slightly ahead of me until we reached the children's section.

The fitting rooms lined either side of an overly bright corridor painted a dingy shade of white. Their louvered half-doors flipped in and out and locked with a metal bolt; as I stood undressed inside, I could see the feet of strangers passing on the other side. My mother chose clothes of all colors, turtlenecks, corduroy pants, outfits to wear to synagogue on Saturdays. "Wait here," she might say, and then leave me to find a different size or a new style. It was chilly, and I'd crouch to my knees and lean my back against the wall to rest.

Clothes shopping was the one activity when I had my mother to myself, when she left my brothers behind and she was the one in charge. I have few memories of the clothes we bought during these trips; much of our search was for things my mother said I needed, and I tried them on to be sure they fit properly. Occasionally, though, there would be something that piqued my enthusiasm. I remember a white pullover made from fuzzy wool that my mother called mohair and agreed to buy, and a blue skirt that she rejected. "It's too tight," she told me, forcing her fingers inside the waistband. "You'll grow out of it too fast."

Once, on a detour to the bathroom, my mother tried to explain to me how to squat over the toilet instead of sitting directly on the seat. This was in lieu of lining the seat with toilet paper, which she usually did for me in the crowded stall. "You can lean over like this," she said, bending her knees and tipping forward. "That way you won't touch the seat." Alone in the stall, I tried to do what she'd told me, but the stance didn't make sense and I was too short anyway. Urine flowed down my legs and into my shoes beneath the arches of my feet. My underpants were warm and sticky. My mother wiped my legs with toilet paper, her movements deft and swift, then led me back to the girls' department where she bought me new underwear. Back in the dressing room, she tore open the package and handed me the white briefs, still folded into a small square. They felt unexpectedly cool against me, fresh and dry.

Occasionally, before we headed home, we stopped in Filene's Basement, on the lower level on the way down to the subway. "Let's see what we can find," my mother might suggest. Here, sloppy racks of dresses abutted tables where items seemed to have been randomly tossed into heaps. Women pushed at one another to rifle through piles of shirts, bins of underwear, stacks of scarves and hats. There was barely room to stand; I'd hover close to my mother as she rummaged, grabbing a sweater or blouse to press against my chest at the shoulders. There were no dressing rooms, so women who wanted to try something on stripped down to their underwear in the middle of us all. I stared at the rolls of pink fat that melted down their sides, and the overstuffed cones of their pasty brassieres. I felt tiny and in danger of being lost, overheated in my coat.

That summer day in Belmont, in that suburban cousin of

Filene's, was different. The store was only blocks away from our new home, and its offerings were condensed onto just two floors. The girls' department was cool and empty; I relished the quiet, other shoppers far away, as I considered my wardrobe choices for my new school. We didn't talk much, my mother and I; we rarely did. But the afternoon comforted me. It was, perhaps, the first bit of soothing I had had in the tumult of the move.

We stand amidst circular racks that turn sluggishly if you push them. More selections line the walls at two levels, interrupted by the entrance to the fitting rooms. My mother is slim, short beside the displays. Looking more at the clothing than at me, she takes one piece after another, then directs me to the dressing rooms to try them on.

My mother is my mirror. Before I form my own opinions, I ease out of the fitting room wearing one possibility after another and wait for her face to tell me how I look. Sometimes she frowns, then approaches me to tug at a shoulder or straighten a collar. When she smiles and nods, I know she is pleased, and I turn to see for myself.

We decide on a knee-length solid maroon pleated skirt with a black button at the waist; a maroon and white plaid kilt, a "wraparound," we call it, complete with an oversized safety pin to hold it closed; a cardigan in the identical shade of maroon, with grosgrain trimming the inner edges where the buttons and buttonholes are; the beige pullover, a "Norwegian ski sweater," my mother tells me; and several pairs of matching maroon knee socks and tights.

I hang back as my mother completes our purchase, then follow a few steps behind as she totes our two crisp white shopping bags out to the parking lot, where she loads them into the back seat of our car and we head home.

When autumn finally arrived, I wore endless permutations of

maroon, reassured by the way my knee-socked calves were clad in the exact shade as the squares in my skirt.

Susan and her mother during a family trip to Washington, D.C.

Dinner at Five

My mother hovers behind me as I slowly starve myself. She serves me dinner at five, an hour before the rest of my family.

That's when I get hungry. I am sixteen, a junior in high school, and by five o'clock I have eaten only half of the eight-hundred calories I allot myself daily. Dinner will take care of the other four-hundred, and after that I will return to my bedroom, finish my homework, and go to sleep.

I have been eating like this since late winter, and now it is April; I have lost at least fifteen pounds. Each morning, I step onto the bathroom scale and watch as the numbers in the window between my toes sway beneath the black dial, then settle somewhere just above one hundred. I am delighted that my jeans are baggy; I gather the fabric behind my thigh into my fist.

My mother doesn't say, "Susan, you must be hungry! Come and have a snack!" She doesn't tell me I look too thin for my frame, or that there are dark circles under my eyes. She doesn't say: "In this family, we eat dinner at six and I expect you at the table."

She is there in the kitchen, turned toward the sink. She is cutting slices from the London broil the rest of my family will eat in an hour, spooning out a serving of simmering peas and a splat of mashed potatoes, arranging them beside each other on my sea-green plate, and bringing them to the table where I sit alone.

It started abruptly, this so-called diet, on a cloudy Saturday when I spent most of the day in my room doing homework. I had plans for the evening, and before going out, I realized I'd only eaten a container of yogurt all day. I took an apple and left. The next morning, I savored the emptiness in my belly.

The part of me that loved to eat shut down. Until that day, I was the one who grabbed the lamb chop bones from my brothers' plates and chewed off the edges of fat; who offered to clean the meat from the chicken carcass, popping the best pieces into my mouth; who stole fingerfuls from the dishes my mother was preparing for supper until she shooed me away with a "Don't pick!" But for a few months in 1970, I had neither appetite nor cravings. The pleasure I took from food was replaced by the gratification of losing myself.

Looking back, I see it was a terrible time. My father, a Harvard-educated chemist with a Ph.D., had lost his job when NASA's headquarters in Cambridge was shut down, and over a six-month period of job applications, interviews, and rejections, he descended into an angry depression. He developed arthritis and spent hours of the day in bed. My mother was never very far away from him, though there was little she could do to help.

I see them standing close together in the living room, the curtains drawn though it is the middle of the day. The mail has arrived, and there is a torn envelope, a letter creased where it had been folded in thirds. My father is shaking his head. My mother stands behind his shoulder, tiny and silent. Then she cups her hand under his elbow and leads him upstairs.

In the afternoons I sit at the desk in my bedroom doing my schoolwork. I do not wonder about my brothers or ask where they are. I lie on my bed on top of the blankets to read.

Close to five, my stomach rumbles. I hear my mother preparing food downstairs, the tinny scrapings of spoons, the staccato dicing of knives, the airy dashes of water as she turns the faucet on and off. The scent of frying onions and cooking meat enters my room. I wait as long as I can, anxious for the meal I will soon allow myself to eat.

My mother has set my regular place at the table, a pockmarked paper napkin folded into a triangle beneath my fork. She expects me.

But what is she thinking? Is she happy about being able to spend time with me alone? Is she annoyed at having to feed me early? Or is she secretly pleased that she can do something special for me?

In the kitchen, my mother does not say, "How was school today?" or, "Do you have a lot of homework?" She does not sit down beside me to rest her feet, to keep me company. I long for conversation; I long for consolation. I eat quickly, clear everything off my plate. I do not taste my food. My mother is whisking, rinsing, cutting, making dinner for the rest of the family. I long for her to stop being occupied. It is her back that I see when I turn my head toward her. I long for her to look at me. I long for her to make me stop.

Instead I stop myself. On a warm day in June, I begin to eat. I come into the kitchen where my parents are seated at the table, reading the newspaper. It is not mealtime but I open the refrigerator and pause for a moment, perusing its contents. I pull out a yellow serving container with half a roasted chicken inside, place it on the table, and remove the lid. I stand as I tear the meat from the bone. Then, my lips still greasy, a crumpled napkin in my hand, I turn toward the cabinets, sampling breakfast cereals and pretzels and black licorice nubs. In the bread drawer I find graham crackers, and with them I eat raisins out of the box. My mother watches me but doesn't say a word.

Not My Father

I am six, and I have done something to make my mother angry; I don't remember what. Maybe I said, "Damn it," which I learned from her but which she's been trying to stop saying. Maybe she said, "Don't say that!" and I spit the words out again.

I know I have been bad but still, I'm surprised to see my mother lose her temper. It is usually my father who gets angry, but he is not at home.

"Go to your room," she says.

Her voice is louder than usual, her words crimped. She is standing in the hallway that runs between the kitchen and the front doorway, wearing a skirt and a tucked-in blouse. I have challenged her somehow, frustrated her, interrupted her. The kitchen behind her is bright, and I can still smell the grilled cheese sandwich she made me for lunch.

When my father yells at me, the words surround me and make me shrivel. They leave me no choice. With my mother it's different. Her words, despite her stern expression, feel meek, and I blow them away.

I turn and head toward the stairs, but instead of going up, I keep on walking and don't look back. I know my mother is still standing there and I don't care that she is watching me. In fact, I'm glad. I continue right out the front door and across the street to my friend Mary Bonano's.

I stand on Mary's front porch and ring the bell. I gaze down the street. When Mary opens the door, I say nothing about what happened. I follow her inside, down the narrow hallway to her bedroom. We play but it's not fun, and soon I go back home.

I think my mother will be standing by the door but she isn't. I hear the rush of water, the clink of dish against dish in the kitchen sink. I wait for her to be mad, to punish me, but she doesn't say anything, doesn't turn around.

We are in Florida, visiting my mother's sister, Shirley, and her family, staying in a nearby hotel. I am around eleven years old, trying on sunglasses in the little shop off the lobby while my parents wait at the counter. I've spotted a pair I want: a single curved band of neon green plastic with a darkened strip of lens running horizontally along the center. They look more like a headband than eyeglasses—no notch for the nose, no hooks around the ears. I like their simplicity and their space-age style. I manage to return to the shop later with my allowance and buy them.

Back in the room, I take the glasses out of the bag to show my parents. Before I can even put them on, my father gets up from his chair. "Those are ridiculous," he says. "They're ugly." I tell him I like them. I tell him I've used my allowance, but he is infuriated. "They are a waste of money. Now go and return them!"

My mother says nothing. I want to model the glasses for her. I think that she might like them on me, but I take the elevator down to the shop and get my money back.

When she married my father, my mother became, above all else, the protector of his equilibrium. She had taken on not only his good looks, his intelligence, his humor, and his charm, but also his spells of moodiness and his unexpected fury. Her character was well suited for the role. She cooked the foods he liked, kept the house tidy to his standards. She, like my brothers and I, was afraid to provoke him, and surrendered herself to his presence.

The price she paid was losing me. The way I saw it, my father was a preferable model; he might be frightening, but at least he was there. I learned his judgment and his disdain, and even in the earliest years, I negated my mother as she negated herself. As a child, I missed her; as I got older I found comfort elsewhere and no longer cared.

It is 1968, and my father has moved to Washington. After six months of unemployment, he was finally offered a job at NASA's headquarters there. Because it is my last year of high school, and my mother is in the final year of a library sciences master's program, my parents decided that my father would rent an apartment and live by himself for a year. After my departure for college, my mother and brothers would join him.

Freed from my father's shadow, I skip school regularly, and forge my mother's signature on notes I write that say I was sick. My boyfriend, Billy, and I drive out to Rockport where we sit on the rocky shore and drink Mateus wine from the bottle. Or we go to his house, empty during the day, smoke a joint and roll around on his bed. I'm not foolhardy; my college applications are in, my grades are good. I have leeway, and I take it.

So on an early winter night when the first snow starts to fall, and Billy grabs my hand, I don't think twice about agreeing to walk all the way home from the movies. We'd taken the bus to the theater, about five miles away in Harvard Square. It is late, maybe eleven o'clock. The sky is low, a blurry gray. The streets are empty; our voices echo along Massachusetts Avenue in the muffled chill. Flakes brush our cheeks and force us to squint. It isn't cold, and we turn our faces toward the clouds.

It is after one a.m. when we arrive, and ours is the only house that is awake. In a glow of light at the back doorway, my mother stands halfway outside. She is alone, her terrycloth bathrobe tied around her waist. The snowflakes are like frantic stars around her head.

I see her and for an instant know everything: her annoyance, her panic, her relief. Her face is pale and serious. "Where *were* you?" she says. "I was worried." Billy looks down, mumbles goodbye. "We walked home," I might have replied, if I said anything at all. I brush past her into the kitchen, then go upstairs to bed.

Womanly Matters

My mother never warned me about my period; I'd heard about it from my friend Laurie, who was a year older, but I didn't know what to expect when I started menstruating at age fourteen. Each day for about a week, I put my soiled panties into the hamper across from the toilet. I didn't mention anything to my mother; I felt a secret shame. And my mother, who took the clothes regularly from the hamper to wash, never said anything to me. The next month, when it started happening again, I understood. I told my mother then, and she gave me sanitary napkins. I wish I could recall the words we exchanged, but at the center of my memory is a young girl who had learned early to find her own way.

Which is how I came to shave my legs. It was fifth grade, and some of the girls were trading ankle socks for nylon stockings. On my own calves, the mesh of the stockings squashed the dark hairs beneath and made them look like nasty little insects. It seemed to me that mine were the only legs with any hairs at all. When I pleaded with my mother to let me shave them, she said I was too young. So one day, in the shower, I took my father's brass razor and soaped up my legs. Drawing the blade from ankle to knee, I made vertical lines through the bubbles, the sound like tearing paper. I never felt guilt; I didn't hide my accomplishment from my mother, and she never acknowledged it. I savored the smoothness and cleanliness of my calves. I had done what had to be done.

It was around that time that I wanted a bra, but my mother declared I didn't need one yet. So I turned to Laurie, who months earlier had proudly raised her shirt to display the training bra her mother had bought her, and not long afterwards its replacement with little cupped mounds. In her bedroom, she rummaged through a drawer and handed me the one she'd outgrown, already grayed with use. The next day I wore it to school, where the boy who sat behind me snapped the strap against my back. My mother eventually found the bra in the hamper, and from then on, we

213

shopped for my bras together.

When I was a junior in high school, I spent my afternoons at my friend Roger Lenneberg's house, along with his girlfriend, Kelly. It was an old Victorian, nestled among trees midway up a steep slope behind the center of town. We gathered there because, with Roger's parents at work, it was empty after school, except for Andy, a boy our age from California who was staying with the Lennebergs. I never knew why he was there, but something about him made me feel protective toward him. We smoked joints, made liverwurst sandwiches, and listened to albums—Crosby, Stills, Nash, and Young; the Beatles; Jefferson Airplane. Soon Roger and Kelly would disappear upstairs and close his bedroom door, leaving Andy and me on the living room couch, where we kissed for what seemed like hours.

One day when I got home, my mother stopped me as I entered the kitchen. She was alone, wearing an apron, mashing potatoes at the stove.

"I got a call from Kelly's mother," she said. "She's concerned that there's no supervision at Roger's." Songs still sang in my mind: "Wooden Ships," "Here Comes the Sun." I thought about Andy, tasted his tongue playing with mine.

"Don't worry about it. It's fine," I said, then headed for the hallway to go upstairs. My mother never asked me about the situation again.

Toward the end of my senior year, my best friend, Wendy, confided that she'd had a discussion with her mother about birth control, and they'd decided she should begin taking the pill when she started college. I had never talked with my mother about sex; I learned about intercourse from a girl named Joyce, the daughter of my parents' friends. I couldn't believe what Joyce was telling me, but I never considered asking my mother if it were true. Shortly after that, my mother bought me a book that she deposited in my bedroom—something about how babies were conceived, and the differences between male and female bodies. I never read it; I thought I already knew what I needed to know. After Wendy told me about the talk with her mother, I wanted to have a similar conversation with mine. One afternoon after school, I approached her in the kitchen as she was preparing supper and dove right in.

"Since I'll be going to college," I said, "I think we should talk about getting me birth control pills." I sat down on one of our yellow vinyl chairs.

My mother stopped what she was doing and turned toward me. She was probably shocked, and likely embarrassed, but all she said was, "You shouldn't even be thinking about that."

We didn't discuss the matter again, but within a month after starting college I *was* on the pill, and by Thanksgiving break, my pubic area was itching severely. All weekend I scratched vehemently. The evening before I was about to leave, in an act that surprises me when I consider it now, I admitted my condition to my mother.

"I can't stop scratching," I said, and in my memory, she answered right away.

"You might have crabs," she said, explaining succinctly what they were and how they were spread.

Horrified, I looked again until I confirmed that she was right, and went to the health clinic as soon as I returned to school. Decades later, when I think about that night, I picture my mother in the dim downstairs. I wonder how she knew about crabs, and what she must have thought about my having them. I remember how calm she was in responding to me, how kind.

The first time my mother talked to me about her sex life with my father was after my father got sick with Alzheimer's. I called her daily to see how he was, and how she was feeling. It was during one of those conversations that she told me, "He wants to have sex all the time. 'Let's have sex,' he'll say."

Growing up, I rarely saw my parents touch. They had friends who held hands or kissed on the lips, but I only saw my parents peck each other's cheeks, when they said goodbye as my father left for work, or when we said "Good *Shabbos*" after lighting the candles on Friday night.

My parents slept with their bedroom door open; we all did—my father didn't like closed doors. I recall at least once walking past their doorway on the way to the bathroom in the early morning and seeing them spooning, my mother facing away from my father, my father curled around her, his head in her hair.

"He says it over and over," she continued. It was the same tone she used to describe his incontinence or the heaviness of his body when she had to support it. "And then when we have it, he forgets and a few minutes later, he wants to do it again."

I didn't know what to say. I let my mother talk, and this time it was I who remained silent.

Weekend Visit

I never told my family that I'd gotten married to Darek, but somehow, by the time he left me eight months later, my mother knew. The weekend after he moved out of my Manhattan apartment, she took a train from Washington to stay with me. She came unaccompanied by my father. I still cannot imagine what she told him or how she managed to arrange the trip.

The problem was Darek's background—it was unthinkable to my father, an observant Jew whose father's family had been slaughtered in Poland, that I date a Polish Catholic. When I began to speak of marriage, my father cut me off.

"Don't tell me! I don't want to hear!" he yelled into the telephone.

My mother was mute on the extension.

So I stopped talking to them about Darek, and when we did get married, it was downtown at City Hall, with Wendy and a man I knew from work as our only witnesses.

I had fallen in love with Darek quickly. I was twenty-six years old, getting my master's degree in filmmaking at Columbia. He was twenty-three, tall and sinewy, recently arrived from Poland to find work in the film industry. He leaned against a brick wall in Soho wearing a long woolen coat and blowing cigarette smoke into the cold air. He spoke with an accent. In bed, he poured champagne onto my belly and licked it off.

Before long, he was living in my apartment. By then I'd graduated and was working as a producer. I paid the rent and bought groceries with the money I made. Through my connections, Darek got a few small jobs as a cinematographer. When he broached the idea of our marrying so that he could get his green card, I readily agreed.

I was thrilled to be sharing my life with this handsome

foreigner. I learned a few words of Polish, and his mother mailed us a white linen tablecloth. We found an immigration lawyer who helped Darek prepare his papers.

Even before the green card arrived in the mail, our lovemaking slowed and I began asking him what was wrong. Within weeks of receiving the document, he announced he was leaving.

"No one will ever love you as much as I do," I said.

"You may be right," he replied.

I was inconsolable, frantic. Although I wouldn't have shared the details with my parents, I must have let my mother know that the relationship had fallen apart. And then, somehow, she was there.

So much of that weekend has vanished from my memory. I remember meeting my mother at Penn Station early on Saturday afternoon. She was fifty-four then, her hair short and still untinged by gray. She wore navy blue slacks and matching blue flats, and carried a small canvas overnight bag. It was March, the sidewalks of New York mostly freed of snow.

Like a drug addict, I fought the relentless urge to call Darek where he was staying with a friend. "I just have to," I'd explain to my mother, disappearing into my bedroom and closing the door behind me. Minutes later, the call over, I'd emerge weeping with hopelessness and frustration. I'd sit down in a chair and cover my face with my palms.

She probably stood up when she saw me, her brow furrowed to reflect my pain. "It'll be all right," she might have said, then waited until I stopped crying. Now I recognize this quiet acceptance, this tolerance without judging, this ability to abide the strongest of emotions in those she loved, as one of her greatest strengths.

When I picture my mother that weekend, she is sitting at my kitchen table. She turns her head over her left shoulder, props her left elbow on the back of her chair to look at me on the other side of the room. I remember a snatch of conversation about replacing that set of hand-me-down kitchen chairs: "You should," my mother said. "You deserve them." A few weeks later, I bought new chairs.

After dinner, we might have watched television. Or maybe we bought the Sunday *New York Times* and sat together over the crossword puzzle. Later, my mother would have changed into a silk nightgown and slippers. Together we would have put sheets and blankets on the spare bed in the living room that doubled as a sofa, and I would have given her a towel. In my mind, I see her walking down the hallway to the bathroom carrying her toiletries in a cloth cosmetics case.

The Sunday before my mother was to leave, we walked to a café on Columbus Avenue where we ordered brunch. We faced each other over a small wooden table, clouds of other people's conversations billowing around us.

Her very presence—this rare demonstration of her love—emboldened me. In a lull in our talk, I tendered a subject I'd never broached before. The words I spoke were not about Darek but about my father.

"You never stood up to him," I said. "How come you never took my side?" I spoke gently, but it was perhaps the most straightforward comment I'd ever made to her.

My mother's eyes glistened red, the way I'd seen them when my father spoke to her harshly, and she looked down. I was sorry right away. "It's fine," I probably said. "Don't worry."

Both of us made it easy to veer away from this subject, and for the duration of our eggs and hash browns, we returned to more banal topics. When we finished our meal, I walked my mother to the subway station at Seventy-Second Street, where we kissed each other on the cheek and said goodbye.

Secrets

My father died never knowing I'd been married to Darek. Silence in our family had come to trump honesty and openness when those options risked inflaming my father's simmering ire. In retrospect, I realize it was my mother on whom that silence weighed most heavily.

I recently came upon a note card she sent me. It was dated July 25, 1983, a little over two years after Darek and I had divorced. I was engaged to my new boyfriend, Paul, who was not only the right religion but also the son of one of my father's colleagues. Paul and I were living together in New York, and, busy with our jobs, we'd gladly relinquished the planning of our wedding to my parents. The ceremony was to be held near their home in Washington, and my mother had taken it upon herself to obtain our marriage license.

The note card was a heavy beige stock, its front adorned with delicate line drawings of purple flowers. Inside, my mother's tidy, distinct script ran slightly upward from left to right. "Dear Sue," she began, the greeting written in blue ink, the rest of the letter in black.

My mother loved note cards. She'd buy them for herself at the museums and shops she and my father visited when they traveled. She used them to accompany gifts, to say thank you or express sympathy, and sometimes to communicate things she preferred not to have to say in person. "I can never have enough," she told me several times, and over the years, I have saved the ones she sent me.

"I've hesitated to say anything over the phone but I do want to tell you what the story is about applying for a license," she wrote in this one. "On the application, there is a question about any previous marriage."

I didn't think much about it then, but rereading the card now, I imagine my mother scheming. She was working as a librarian, so probably dealt with the license on her lunch break. In my mind she was efficient and directed, clutching the handles of her leather purse in one hand as she headed to her car.

"I suggested to Dad that I would apply for it," she wrote. "I'm trying to work it that way without making a big issue about it."

My mother and I rarely spoke alone, just the two of us. It was my father who greeted me when they called, told stories, asked questions, my mother inserting a few words now and then on the extension. If she had asked to have a private conversation with me, my father would probably have said, "What for?"

"Can you somehow let me know the date of your marriage and divorce without raising any questions from Dad?" the letter went on. I remember I called my mother at work with the information she needed to complete the application. I didn't think of it as deception; it didn't occur to me that there might have been other ways of responding to my father's closed-mindedness. I followed my mother's lead, complicit without a second thought.

Over the years, there were other things we didn't tell my father. When my daughter Sofie was born, my mother sent me a check for several thousand dollars from an account she said my father wouldn't see. And no one had the courage to tell him that my brother Eric had converted to Islam. Before my father was entirely lost in his Alzheimer's disease, Eric expressed a wish to reveal the truth about his life. My mother and I discussed the possible outcomes. She felt my father might be able to accept the revelation and let it go, as he did many things at that time; I feared that the knowledge would become the only thing he thought about, even if he didn't fully understand. In the end, Eric decided not to say anything.

After my father's death, my mother said her sister, Shirley, berated her for all those times she'd been unable to confront him, for coddling him with ignorance. She told her it was wrong, and my mother confessed that she had felt guilty keeping secrets from him. But the way I see it, she was doing whatever she needed to sidestep my father's rage—or maybe worse, a dark depression. She was not only protecting my father, she was shielding her children. Only now do I recognize how alone that left her.

I Love You

"Did I tell you?" my mother is saying. "Now, whenever David and I leave each other, we say, 'I love you.'"

I am talking to her on the telephone, and yes, she has told me this several times of late. She and my youngest brother, David, have taken to stating their love. She says she was inspired by my family; unlike when I was growing up, we tell one another "I love you" easily and often. And when my daughters talk to my mother on the phone, they end their conversations with the phrase.

"I got it from Sofie and Ariel," my mother says. "David and I decided it was a good idea. It's nice."

It wasn't until my father became ill in his late seventies that he started declaring his love verbally. "I love your mother so much," he'd tell me, or, "I'm so proud of you." When I was a child, such sentiments were rarely spoken. There was anger, yes, and fear and worry, but love, while assumed, remained unexpressed.

When I became a mother, things were different with my daughters. There was a lot of hugging and touching, and Paul and I were so overcome with emotion for our girls that we couldn't help but tell them of our love over and over. I hadn't decided consciously that it should be this way; an instinctive, pervasive, maternal love was released inside me, and I was delighted to let it out. It was only natural, then, that Sofie and Ariel would speak their feelings in return, to us and to others, including their grandparents.

As for me, I never said "I love you" to my parents. Even as I got older and reconciled many of my sentiments toward them, I couldn't say the words. They stuck in my throat, and I swallowed them down.

My mother and I talk on the phone almost daily now. I've come to understand her more fully, to admire her, to like her, and she is relaxed and open with me. Once in a while, she says, "I love you, Sue." She seems a little embarrassed, awkward, but I can hear that she is smiling, and I answer, "I love you, too." I say it quickly, with no real feeling attached. I have yet to say it first, and I know that when she is gone, I will regret not having said it more. I know that if I did, she would respond without hesitation, with relief and joy. I begin sometimes, but there is a split second of choice, when I succumb to the easier path and let my discomfort vanquish my will. A part of me is still frozen, stubborn, holding on to something old, refusing to let go.

Toothpick Girl

"Can I have that when you're dead?"

As I point at the little wooden figure, my mother turns from her breakfast to see what I am talking about. I am visiting her shortly after my father died, helping her go through the piles of paperwork that have accumulated since things became dire.

I see a flicker of dismay at my question, quickly replaced by a half smile. I will realize much later that it is a bit of a dare, what I'm asking, forcing the focus from the hugeness of death to an inconsequential decision about an old doll.

"Why wait?" my mother says, meeting my challenge. She takes a sip of her coffee.

The figure stands about four inches tall, a handcrafted woman wearing a wide-brimmed hat whose paint is peeling off. Her body is carved in the shape of a dark blue dress that is cinched at the waist. Her stubby arms rest on the handle of a wheelbarrow whose wheels are no bigger than nickels.

I remember her from the Belmont house where she sat on the small shelves above the kitchen table. The salt and pepper shakers were there, too, and my father's pipe and tobacco, so he could reach them easily after supper for a smoke. Year after year, she was silent witness to our meals.

Now, here in my mother's kitchen, she looks lost beside the sugar bowl on a cluttered tray. I bring her home and place her in my own kitchen, on the windowsill over the sink. I fill her wheelbarrow with toothpicks.

I love her unassuming lines and simple roundness. She is a relic of my past, my memory made tangible.

My Mother's Leg

We are visiting my mom because of her left hand, but it is the image of her right leg that stays with me.

She fell a few days earlier, walking downhill on wet leaves near her home. She is eighty-two, healthy and upbeat, but she walks cautiously, reaching out for support from whatever is nearby, especially when she's rounding a corner. "I should have been more careful," she says of the moments before her fall.

My mother didn't report the incident to me for two days. On the phone, she told me she fell forward. The gloves she was wearing tore from the impact, and she scraped her knee through her fleece pants. "My nose was bleeding," she said. A man driving by stopped to see if she was hurt. "He had his young son in the backseat," she went on, "so I felt all right taking him up on his offer to bring me home."

In my mind, she hits the ground flat like a board. The picture of her lying face down on the sidewalk, blood flowing from her nose, makes me shudder.

A visit to her doctor the next day determined no bones were broken. "I was lucky," she said. "I find it hard to believe because my hand is so swollen." Which is why Paul and I decided to make the trip from New York.

She stands behind the glass door to her house watching as we make our way up the walk, and kisses us each on the cheek when we enter. She wears tan corduroys and one of my father's turtlenecks beneath a coral-colored cotton sweater I gave her years ago. Her short gray hair provides little contrast to her pale complexion. You can see the bruises on the sides of her nose where her glasses were shoved into her face. She is smiling, and I am glad to see she seems fine.

Her hand, however, emerges from her sleeve like a bruised fruit. It is blue and gray, so bloated no knuckles are visible. My mother says she isn't using it, but I catch her repeatedly involving it

225

in activities alongside her right hand, balancing the side of the orange juice bottle, or holding the edge of a baking sheet of potatoes. "Don't do that!" I yell, but she ignores me.

My mother is as caught as I am between the reality of her age and the memory of who she always was. Her fall dislodges us both, and all weekend, I observe her. Because of the cold, she dresses in layers that thicken her silhouette. For most of her life, my mother, who is an inch or so over five feet tall, was petite and slender; she tucked her blouses into her slacks. She had a secret stash of miniature chocolate bars that she ate watching television at night— "to keep my weight up," she explained once when I discovered the bag. Now her belly protrudes roundly onto her lap when she sits. I notice the way the sides of her cheeks hang as if tired, and the blurriness of the line from her chin to her neck.

I don't see my mother's leg until the next morning, when she decides to change the Band-Aid that is protecting the scrape on her right knee. She is standing, and I am sitting nearby on the edge of her bed. She is wearing her nightgown, and has to lift its bottom edge up to her thigh to keep it out of the way. The scrape looks like a child's skinned knee, softened from the Bacitracin she's been using.

The way her nightgown is raised, I can see a side view of almost the entire length of her leg. It stands rooted to the floor, the skin the faintest pink, sprinkled with freckles and cherry red spots, and slightly mottled, especially close to the top. The calf is cone-shaped, its skin smooth and taut, ending abruptly at the lumpy circle of her knee. The thigh is a larger cone, mushier and less defined. The only time I've seen my mother's bare legs is when she wears her bathing suit, but I've never paid them any attention. Now her right leg is displayed before me. I study it as she works to apply her Band-Aid. I examine it for the signs of age, for flaccidness or decay. I think briefly of my father, dead almost a year.

Then it strikes me: this is my own leg. I recognize the color and shape, the tone of the flesh. I've never identified my body with my mother's; hers, I thought, was finer, more delicate. I always considered myself stocky. But her leg, I finally recognized, is my leg. It isn't fat; it is solid and functional. But it isn't elegant, it isn't beautiful. It stands on the floor the way a leg is meant to do. For an instant, it makes me sad, this sudden nearness to my mother's body, but I dispel the feeling, retaining only the image. The limb, so human, irregular and too short, the color like pearl.

Before Me

"You would have loved your grandmother Ida," my father told me many times when I was growing up. He was speaking of my mother's mother, who died several months after I was born. My parents had described her to me as under five feet tall and a heavy smoker, but other than that, I was left to imagine why she was so wonderful.

In fact, I was left to imagine much of my mother's past. She wasn't a storyteller when we were younger, and shared little about her childhood. And I wasn't curious enough to ask.

Then in 2002 I received a copy of a book compiled by my Aunt Shirley, filled with photographs, facts, and anecdotes about our extended family. I turned directly to the section on my mother's immediate branch, filling in details I'd never known. With them, along with my own imagination, I reconstructed pieces of my mother's early life.

In 1929, when she was two, her family moved from Canton, Massachusetts, to Inwood, in Upper Manhattan, where her father, Sam Wenesky, worked as a salesman for the Plymouth Rubber Company. My mother was a curly-headed little girl, close with Shirley. Together they would roller skate and jump "sisters," the two sharing one rope in the park across from their building. They'd stand outside the Loew's Inwood movie theater on Dyckman Street asking passersby to purchase tickets for them. In winter, they huddled bundled up on the fire escape outside their bedroom window, watching sledders on Hillside Avenue, blowing air like smoke into the chilly afternoon.

Their father was often away on business, but when he was around, he made them laugh and they clamored for his attention. They played restaurant with an easel-style blackboard in their dark living room, insisting he order his dinner before the family sat down to eat. On Sundays, they took walks with him along the East River, accompanied by an uncle and the uncle's dog, Tusca.

Then their father died. It was from a botched hospital procedure, when my mother was only ten. I first learned this as a young girl, and the idea that a father could die both horrified and fascinated me. My mother keeps a framed photograph of him and her mother on the tabletop beside her Sabbath candlesticks. It's a wedding shot: my grandmother wears a white dress and veil and clasps a bouquet of white flowers with both hands; my grandfather towers over her, a broad-shouldered man with fleshy cheeks in a dark jacket and a brimmed black hat.

Prompted by my aunt's book, I asked my mother about this stage of her parents' life, and she told me that if her father hadn't died, Ida would have left him. "He was a traveling salesman..." she said by way of explanation. She said my grandmother had torn his face out of all her other photographs. Then she pointed to their wedding photo. "Did I ever tell you? One time the picture fell off the table, and the crack in the glass went right between them."

Ida, Shirley, and my mother were left destitute. They returned to Canton, where they lived with one of Sam's brothers, who was widowed and sick. They received welfare and packages of used clothing, and the sisters had to stand in line for free milk. "We hated it," my mother told me. "We'd cry that we didn't want to go."

Soon they were joined by a cousin, Syl, who had left home because she didn't get along with her mother. The four of them had to share a single bed. My mother said they slept horizontally side by side, and now I envision them there, their feet hanging over the edge.

My mother always had a sweet voice; she loved singing show tunes while I was growing up. When she was in high school, she entered a talent contest at the local movie theater, the Canton Strand, and won with her performance of "Melancholy Baby." The promoters owned a radio station, where the winners of the talent contests sang. I picture her in some old-fashioned sound booth, with red lipstick and hair grown long and held off her forehead by a barrette, a smile crinkling her eyes.

Unlike Shirley, my mother attended college, thanks to an uncle who came into enough money to help. She lived with her mother and sister in Canton, and went to Simmons, in Boston. After she graduated, she got a job working for the telephone company.

When she was twenty-five, a mutual friend introduced her to my father. "I really liked him," my mother told me. "I knew right away I wanted to marry him."

The life they created together was strategic and tidy; all things had their place in our home, with no room to spare for what didn't belong. I remember us laughing at the dinner table, but if my brothers and I got too silly, my father would say, "That's enough," and we'd stop. What I think I longed for in my own childhood was some of the messiness of my mother's, the struggles and the flaws that were, nonetheless, cushioned by warmth and love.

Inwood

I drive across the Henry Hudson Bridge and get off the parkway at Dyckman Street, an exit I have always associated with my mother but never taken. It is mid-August, blue-skied and not too hot, and my mother is spending a long weekend with Paul and me. Our outing this afternoon is to drive through Inwood, the section of northern Manhattan where her family lived for eight years when my mother was between the ages of two and ten.

In an old black-and-white photograph I have of her taken on the sidewalk of a New York City street, my mother must be about three years old. She is dressed in what looks to be a snowsuit—puffy pants and a jacket zippered up to her chin—with a woolen cap pulled over her forehead and ears. She is flanked by Shirley and another young girl; a woman behind them identified as "Florence from Louisville" encircles the three glum-faced girls with outstretched arms and smiles into the camera from beneath the brim of her hat. My mother looks down, the shadow of whoever is taking the picture obliterating her feet.

Today, she is sitting beside me in the passenger seat; Paul is behind us observing in silence. My mother holds the map I printed out earlier but is not looking at it. She wears cream-colored linen pants, a pink t-shirt, and tan lace-up walking shoes. As we approach her old neighborhood, she straightens, leans forward, turns her head from side to side.

"Nagle Avenue, yes, Nagle Avenue." She points out the window. "We walked here," she says. "We went to the movies there."

Her voice gets clearer, a little louder, as we continue to drive. "And Thayer Street, I remember Thayer Street."

On a corner is a boxy tan brick structure with metal window frames painted crimson: P.S. 152. "My school!" my mother says. "I can't believe it's still standing! And here's Ellwood Street, where the Rosenthals used to live."

When I was a child, our family made several visits to New York City, where we saw the Statue of Liberty, the Guggenheim Museum, and the Empire State Building. We traveled by car from the suburbs of Boston, and each time, we stayed with the Rosenthals in their apartment on Ellwood Street.

"We're going to Aunt Eve's," we'd say, even though Eve Rosenthal was my mother's mother's cousin, not anyone's aunt. The building we see driving by with my mother today is just as I remember it: concrete brick with a fire escape climbing its side, near the street corner where what is now a bodega was once, I am sure, a toy store. Aunt Eve's apartment was on the ground floor, and I remember peering through the grating outside the open window to watch street life so different from our quiet sidewalks back home.

Whenever we arrived at Aunt Eve's, one of the first things she did was to take my brother Eric and me to the toy store downstairs and tell us we could pick out anything we wanted. This was not something our parents would ever do; they were frugal and a treat for us kids would be considered unnecessary and wasteful. As I trailed a few steps behind Aunt Eve, the noise of the traffic, the shouts of strangers, the closeness of so many people—let alone the promise of a new toy—thrilled me.

Once we chose a container of small plastic monkeys whose tails curved up into a spiral. Back in the apartment, Eric and I spent hours playing with them, giggling as we hung them from the cords of the venetian blind that was drawn up over the window, my mother sitting with Aunt Eve at a table behind us talking about people I didn't know. There was a lightness in the air; we were on vacation, and Eric and I could play undisturbed, perching on the back of a plush armchair, something we wouldn't have been permitted to do at home.

As we drive through the streets of Inwood, this memory

springs to life. It comforts me, excites me, reminds me of the little girl I once was, but I don't say anything about it. I deliberately withhold myself from my mother, unable to let out words and feelings that would be easy to share with others. It is a reaction, I believe, to her passivity of the past. When we talk now, she is open-minded and pleasant, never cruel or critical. But there is something inside me that remains reserved. Perhaps I am being cautious, unwilling to face a response from her that might be inadequate or disappointing. Mixed into that, I can't deny, is an anger I wish I didn't have. In another family's car, there might have been laughter and tears, but in ours there is quiet. That flicker of awareness is like swallowing something sharp.

Then we arrive at her old apartment building, 34-54 Hillside Avenue. It is red brick, with a terracotta-tiled walk leading from the street to an arched glass doorway. We park the car and get out.

My mother gazes up at the rows of windows stacked one above the next. Then she turns and looks across the street. "We used to play there," she says, directing our attention to a sloping, overgrown park enclosed by a chain-link fence. I try to picture her there, tossing a ball with Shirley, running back home down the hill when it was time for dinner. I try to imagine her, dressed in her winter jacket and hat, going in and out of the glass doors. But I cannot bring her to life.

"Come on, let me take your picture," says Paul.

When we get home, Paul brings the image up on his computer screen. In it, my mother stands in her characteristic posture: legs slightly apart, shoulders a little rounded, her head tilted the tiniest bit upward. She is at the end of the walkway, in front of the doors. I am standing on her right, and it looks as if her arm is reaching out to touch my back.

Susan and her mother at the Hillside Avenue apartment building

Bad News

"I have some bad news about Aunt Shirley," my mother says. "Call me when you get this message." From "bad" on, her words start to melt. I know how her face must have looked, her lips quivering, her eyes turning red. My stomach clenches.

Aunt Shirley, my mother's only sibling, three years older than she. I dial my mother's number. "What?" I say.

She tells me that Aunt Shirley went out for a walk, the neighbor's truck hit her... "Well, the upshot is that she passed away," she says, her voice calm now, even.

"It's how she would have wanted to go," my mother says. She tells me she spoke to my cousin Heidi, Shirley's daughter, and learned that Shirley was conscious when she arrived at the hospital, and that her heart stopped two hours later when they were intubating her in preparation for surgery.

"She would have hated rehab," my mother says.

"It's like I keep forgetting, but then it hits me," she tells me later. There was no funeral; my aunt was cremated, according to her wishes. My mother decides she'll say *kaddish* for thirty days. "I'm the only one who observes the rituals," she says. "It'll make me feel better."

A memorial is being planned, to be held in an art museum in Jacksonville, not far from Shirley's house. It's what they did when her husband, my Uncle Ted, died decades ago.

"I always knew Shirley had a better brain than I did," my mother says. She is telling me that Heidi has begun to go through my aunt's house, and found that Shirley had made notes of many of her wishes. "She was really smart," my mother says, "but I never realized she was so organized. It makes me feel like I should be doing that. I have to be better prepared."

My mother keeps saying she's okay, but I know she's sad. She got a call from a cousin she hadn't talked to since she was a child. "For a moment I thought, 'Oh, I have to call Shirley to tell her," my mother says. "But it's okay. I'm okay." I imagine her alone in the house, without my father, without her sister to talk to on the phone.

My two brothers and I call my mother often. We make sure she's all right, ask her how things are going, keep her updated on our lives. But none of us, my mother explains, replaces her sister. "I talked to her about everything, things you wouldn't be interested in."

But then she says: "I may be calling you more, when I feel like talking to Shirley and she's not there. It's not that different, a sister and a daughter."

"That's fine," I say.

Stand-in sister: I like the idea.

Hello

"Hello."

For a moment I am disoriented. It is afternoon, and I am sitting at my desk. I am expecting to hear my sister-in-law's voice, but it is my mother who answers the telephone.

"Oh, sorry," I say. "I was trying to call Stephanie."

"Oh, well…"

I already spoke to my mother this morning, so there isn't much to say. "Everything okay?" I ask.

"Yes, fine."

"Okay, then. I'll talk to you later." We hang up and I call Stephanie.

Later it happens again. I am intending to call Paul, but there she is.

"Hello?"

"What was I thinking? I meant to call Paul."

And then a third time in the evening, when I think I am calling a friend: "Hello."

This time I am alarmed. What am I doing?

"Sorry," I say. "I don't know what's going on with me."

"That's okay," my mother replies. "You must really want to talk to me."

If it were anyone else, I'd be mortified. I don't remember dialing my mother's number. My finger acted apart from my mind, on what impulse I have no idea. I hear the television in the background, picture my mother with the cordless phone in the den. Has she infiltrated my subconscious?

"Anyway, it's always good to hear your voice," she says.

I hang up again, but for the rest of the night, I think about my mother, satisfied that, in spite of myself, I've let her know she is on my mind.

Susan's mother in her kitchen

My Mother Singing

It is the afternoon of our twenty-fifth wedding anniversary party; our sixty guests line the tables that fill the dining room of a Turkish restaurant. Between the salad and the main course, my mother slides her chair back and stands. In a voice that is as sweet and melodious as I remember from my childhood, with an edge of hoarseness that has come with age, she sings the lyrics she's written for Paul and me to the tune of "I'm in Love with a Wonderful Guy."

> *I expect every one of you here to agree,*
> *that Susan and Paul are the best you will see*

The gathering quiets and turns toward my mother. She seems so small, planted in the center of the group, directing her words around the room but returning repeatedly to meet my eyes.

> *And you'll say I'm naïve as the mother of Sue*
> *To think she can do all the things she can do*

My mother has done this before; at parties, she and my father would often sing duets of familiar tunes with new words capturing the person they were celebrating.

"I might try to write new lyrics to a song," she told me over the telephone weeks before our party, "but I may have to read them because my voice isn't what it used to be."

"That's okay," I said. "No one will mind."

And here she is. She is dressed in black flowing pants and a black turtleneck, with a multicolored, hand-sewn jacket she bought at a crafts fair. A strand of pearls with matching earrings and well-blotted red lipstick are her only adornments. There is a hint of blush in her usually pale cheeks.

Sue and Paul are a most happy couple
Paul and Sue are a really great team

I am filled with a mixture of pride and discomfort, and I cannot move. My eyes fix on my mother, and the rest of the room falls away. I try not to picture her alone at home composing this song. I try not to think about my father, who would be singing beside her if he were alive. I consider the courage it takes to sing to all these strangers, then realize that for my mother, it is a source of joy.

Susan and Paul—c'est magnifique,
Paul and Sue are extraordinaire!
If you'll excuse an expression I'll use:
They're in love, they're in love, and because they're in love,
We're in love with a wonderful pair!

The restaurant is still, save for the shift of a few chairs and the tinkling of plates and silverware in the kitchen. Cars pass on the street outside, and there is the scent of grilling fish. My mother's voice wavers a little, and a few times she stumbles over her words, but the song soars around the room.

Still Here

*S*usan

For my mother's eighty-third birthday, I decided to compile all the stories about her that I was working on in our writing group. I thought I could bind them nicely and give them to her as a gift. But when I shared my idea one Thursday morning, Joan questioned me.

"Aren't you worried that some of what you say will upset her?"

I'd already considered this. Sure, there were some initial condemnations, some unhappy memories, but wouldn't my mother be glad when she got to the end, where I expressed my delight in our newly close relationship? Plus, she was aware of her inadequacies in my earlier years. We'd discussed them on occasion; she had her regrets, I knew, but I thought she'd made peace with them.

"I don't know," Joan insisted. "It might hurt her to see it in writing."

So I found another birthday gift. For the moment, I decided not to take the risk.

My mother had known I was writing about her since the beginning. In keeping with her character, she rarely inquired about the book, never asked to see anything.

Nevertheless, and in spite of Joan's warning, I wanted her to read what I'd written. I wanted her to know how I saw things—how I saw her. I wanted her to feel good about us now.

And so for her eighty-fourth birthday, I did give her my stories. A few days later, she told me on the phone that she'd enjoyed them. She said she didn't remember some of what happened the way I'd written it, but was interested in my point of view. She never mentioned being hurt or saddened by how I'd portrayed her as a young mother, nor flinched at any of my revelations about myself.

It is a great relief to me to have had the chance to tell her all the ways I've been thinking about her, and to have done so in the best way that I could.

*J*oan

Three months before I joined the writers group, my husband underwent cancer surgery and was hospitalized for a frightening, exhausting week. My mother had been dead for eleven years, but in a way that I find difficult to explain, I often felt her near me. I could sense her hovering around, as if she were offering the support I so badly needed. I don't believe in spirits, ghosts, or messages from the great beyond, and I never told anyone about this.

Before I began exploring my memories of my mother, I'm not sure how often I thought of her. But in writing about her, I plunged into her past: the way she looked, smelled, and spoke from the time I was a child until just weeks before her death. I recreated half-forgotten incidents, looked at old photographs of her, examined the memorabilia she'd left behind. I listened to her voice on tape telling stories of her life. For several years, she was a near-constant presence in my life.

Now I wonder: what if I hadn't spent those years writing and rewriting my memories of my mother? Would she still be as vivid a presence in my life? Or would she have faded away?

Lori

When I finally began writing about my mother, I would picture her in an armchair, dressed in a white button-down over black pants, smoking a cigarette. She'd act engrossed in what I had to say. But, as it happened, my mother being my mother, soon she'd lean forward, extinguish her cigarette in the antique ashtray on her lap, and begin to talk about her past. Day after day, I recreated those scenes, and she would respond to me in that crisp voice of hers. At times she was sweet, at times funny and caring. Sometimes she was enraged. That was the voice that I thought would be the loudest, but I was wrong. I hadn't expected to find such variation in her tone, and suddenly all I wanted to do was listen.

These women, these writers I'd come to trust, now my remarkable friends, listened with me. V.S. Naipaul writes about "a sifting through of impulses, ideas, and references that become more multifarious as one grows older..." We were all sifting together.

Would I have eventually written about my mother without them? I think so, yet I would have missed so much: the tenderness I feel for the three of them and their mothers, as well as those particular truths that often materialized during our discussions in the dining room. Joan, Vicki, and Susan all came with me as I stumbled upon hard moments of my past, and whether they knew it or not, at some indeterminate point, they were also with me when I arrived at what I'd yearned for from the start, a quiet place where I could find some peace.

$\mathcal{V}$icki

I used to think my relationship with my mother had ended with her death. Once she was gone, all that we had ever said to each other, the things we had done together, the memories I carried of my life with her, were finite.

I used to believe that a memory was fixed; the past was concrete, stable, constant. What had gone before could not be altered.

When I decided to write about my mother and me, I thought it would be like taking dictation. I would only have to record what my memory spoke. I was sure I already knew the stories I would tell.

But each week, as the four of us gathered to read and listen, the responses to my writing would often lead to questions that slid behind assumptions and around the familiar, to expose details, nuances, fragments of memory I had previously disregarded. My stories began to expand; they spread wide.

Writing together, we helped one another see our own stories from varying points of view. I was able to push aside guilt and shame. Good mother, bad daughter; bad mother, good daughter—it did not matter, it was not the point. As we wrote, it was only who we were, who we are.

As I change, so does my perception of my mother. As time passes, the memories that keep her alive are washed in a new light. Our relationship is ongoing; it is a wellspring.

Front: Lori Toppel and Vicki Addesso. Back: Susan Hodara and Joan Potter

Vicki Addesso began writing memoir in 1998 and is working on a collection of short stories. Her work has been published by *damselfly press*.

Susan Hodara is a journalist, memoirist, and teacher. Her short memoirs have appeared in a variety of literary journals and anthologies; one was nominated for a Pushcart Prize. Her articles are published in the *New York Times*, *Communication Arts*, and other publications. She has taught memoir writing since 2003.

Joan Potter is a writer and teacher whose work has been published in magazines, newspapers, literary journals, and anthologies. Her most recent book is *African American Firsts: Famous, Little-Known and Unsung Triumphs of Blacks in America* (Kensington, 2009).

Lori Toppel's novel, *Three Children* (Summit Books, 1992), was nominated for the Hemingway Foundation/PEN Award. Her stories and essays have appeared in such journals as *Antioch Review* and *Del Sol Review*.

The authors all live and work in Westchester County, NY.

Made in the USA
Lexington, KY
14 April 2013